Copyright © 2025 Patrick Murphy
All rights reserved.

No part of this publication may be reproduced, stored in a retrieval system, or transmitted in any form or by any means—electronic, mechanical, photocopying, recording, or otherwise—without the prior written permission of the author, except in the case of brief quotations used in reviews or articles.

Scripture quotations marked (ESV) are taken from the English Standard Version, copyright © 2001 by Crossway. Used by permission. All rights reserved.

Scripture quotations marked (NIV) are taken from the Holy Bible, New International Version®, copyright © 1973, 1978, 1984, 2011 by Biblica, Inc.® Used by permission. All rights reserved.

Scripture quotations marked (NLT) are taken from the Holy Bible, New Living Translation, copyright © 1996, 2004, 2015 by Tyndale House Foundation. Used by permission of Tyndale House Publishers, a Division of Tyndale House Ministries, Carol Stream, Illinois 60188. All rights reserved.

Scripture quotations marked (AMP) are taken from the Amplified® Bible, copyright © 1954, 1958, 1962, 1964, 1965, 1987 by The Lockman Foundation. Used by permission. All rights reserved. (www.Lockman.org)

ISBN: 979-8-9985487-0-3

First Edition

Illustrations and cover design by Patrick Murphy

Printed in the United States of America

For more information, visit: 133ONE.com

Intro

The seeds for this book were sown as daily devotional texts for my boys and a few of their friends, fondly known as the "young men." Once a week, I'd include a simple, old-school sketch—hand-drawn with ink pens and Sharpie markers. Over time, the audience for these weekly texts and drawings grew to include friends and family.

Text by text, drawing by drawing, this book was born.

The devotionals spring from curiosity and a deep desire to understand the unique fingerprint of our Creator—revealed through Scripture, His creation, and the everyday moments that shape us.

One Thirty Three One is a collection of 133 drawings and paintings, and one testimony, inspired by *Psalm 133:1 (ESV)* "How good and pleasant it is when brothers dwell in unity."

This verse holds a sacred place in our hearts. In 2022, we lost our eldest son in a river accident. Though the pain is deep, Psalm 133:1 reminds us of the promise of eternity—that we will dwell together again, forever united in heaven.

This book is for the young, the old, and everyone in between. Whether you're full of faith, full of questions, or somewhere in between, may these pages help you rediscover childlike wonder and stir your heart toward something greater

Thank you for taking this journey with me.

—*Patrick Murphy*

Stripes

Zebras are known for their stripes. The unique pattern develops in-utero in the eighth month. They are born with light brown streaks that darken to black as they mature. Similar to a human fingerprint, no two zebras share the same pattern. Although humans don't have stripes, if you spend enough time with someone, you will begin to discover all of the things that make them uniquely and wonderfully made.

"For you formed my inward parts; you knitted me together in my mother's womb. I praise you, for I am fearfully and wonderfully made. Wonderful are your works; my soul knows it very well. My frame was not hidden from you, when I was being made in secret, intricately woven in the depths of the earth. Your eyes saw my unformed substance; in your book were written, every one of them, the days that were formed for me, when as yet there was none of them."
Psalm 139:13-16 ESV

"Grab the bull by the horns" - This expression most likely originated in the American West where it was a common, but dangerous cowboy practice to wrestle a young bull to the ground. This involved leaping from a running horse onto the back of the bull, grabbing the horns in a vice-like headlock and wrestling the animal to the ground. The cowboy would then keep the animal pinned while his compadres tended to the needs of the bull. The idiom is now most commonly used when referencing a problem that we need to face head on. So often in life we view this as something we need to buck up and do alone. I am reminded that the cowboy had the help of his horse and fellow ranch hands to execute his dangerous, but necessary task. You may be put in a situation where you need to grab the bull by the horns, but it is important to remember you do not have to face it alone.

No Bull

"So do not fear, for I am with you; do not be dismayed, for I am your God. I will strengthen you and help you; I will uphold you with my righteous right hand."
Isaiah 41:10 NIV

Servant Leader

At a whopping 22 months, elephants have the longest gestation period of any mammal. Baby elephants are born nearly blind and must rely on their mom and her close-knit herd for every need.
Males typically don't leave the group until they are teenagers, while females remain with their mothers for life. Today, I reflect on the mother elephant's example of servant leadership. It serves as a good reminder that the important things in life are not easy, but they are certainly worth doing—and doing well.

"Do nothing from selfish ambition or conceit, but in humility count others more significant than yourselves. Let each of you look not only to his own interests, but also to the interests of others. " Philippians 2:3-4 ESV

93 Million Miles

There are roughly 100 billion stars in the Milky Way galaxy. If you could surf through space, logging one star per second, you would count a whopping 31,536,000 per year. That means it would take 3,171 years to count them all. Now take into consideration that God knows each one by name. Even cooler than that is the star He placed closest to the Earth: the Sun. We orbit in the sweet spot, roughly 93 million miles away. Any closer, and things would warm up significantly; any farther, and we would have nothing but frozen tundra.

A lesser-known fact is that Jupiter acts as a shield for the delicate rock we call home. Jupiter, with its enormous gravitational field, deflects comets and asteroids that would otherwise smash into the Earth.

I stand in awe of these things I take for granted each day—things that are essential to our very existence.

"For by him all things were created, in heaven and on earth, visible and invisible, whether thrones or dominions or rulers or authorities—all things were created through him and for him. And he is before all things, and in him all things hold together."
Colossians 1:16-17 ESV

Orcas can be differentiated and identified by their unique dorsal fin, their saddle marking, and most accurately by the scars they have accumulated over their lifetime. In life we will face many trials, some will leave visible scars, while others, often the deepest hurts, scar our very hearts. I was reminded this morning that Jesus was scarred for our transgressions. Thomas could see the surface wounds, but we may never fully appreciate the heart level wounds that Jesus suffered on our behalf.

Scars

"Now Thomas, one of the Twelve, called the Twin, was not with them when Jesus came. So the other disciples told him, "We have seen the Lord." But he said to them, "Unless I see in his hands the mark of the nails, and place my finger into the mark of the nails, and place my hand into his side, I will never believe." Eight days later, his disciples were inside again, and Thomas was with them. Although the doors were locked, Jesus came and stood among them and said, "Peace be with you." Then he said to Thomas, "Put your finger here, and see my hands; and put out your hand, and place it in my side. Do not disbelieve, but believe." Thomas answered him, "My Lord and my God!" Jesus said to him, "Have you believed because you have seen me? Blessed are those who have not seen and yet have believed." John 20:24-29 ESV

Whisper

Whisper - typically used between two confidants. It is a quiet voice that requires closeness. It is the tone in which secretes and dreams are shared. It is the sound of earnest prayers and not yet realized hopes.   It is the still small voice that we approach our Creator, and it is the breeze stirring the stillness that He answers us.

"And he said, "Go out and stand on the mount before the Lord." And behold, the Lord passed by, and a great and strong wind tore the mountains and broke in pieces the rocks before the Lord, but the Lord was not in the wind. And after the wind an earthquake, but the Lord was not in the earthquake. And after the earthquake a fire, but the Lord was not in the fire. And after the fire the sound of a low whisper." 1 Kings 19:11-12 ESV

Shield of Faith

I was contemplating the gift of faith the other day. One of my favorite verses describes faith as a shield. In my drawings, I often depict this shield as a red umbrella. Problems have a way of expanding quickly, becoming much more than we can handle on our own.

From a distance, a problem may seem small, but as it gets closer, we realize it's far too much to face solo.

"Therefore take up the whole armor of God, that you may be able to withstand in the evil day, and having done all, to stand firm. Stand therefore, having fastened on the belt of truth, and having put on the breastplate of righteousness, and, as shoes for your feet, having put on the readiness given by the gospel of peace. In all circumstances take up the shield of faith, with which you can extinguish all the flaming darts of the evil one; and take the helmet of salvation, and the sword of the Spirit, which is the word of God,"
Ephesians 6:13-17 ESV

Action - Reaction

Isaac Newton
"And to every action, there is always an equal and opposite, or contrary, reaction."

The law of conservation of energy states:
"Energy cannot be created or destroyed, but can only be transferred from one form to another."

I love how the energy transfer we observe in a puddle jump demonstrates a masterful Creator, who alone holds the keys to the mystery behind energy itself.

"Before the mountains were brought forth, or ever you had formed the earth and the world, from everlasting to everlasting you are God. You return man to dust and say, "Return, O children of man!" For a thousand years in your sight are but as yesterday when it is past, or as a watch in the night."
Psalm 90:2-4 ESV

Lonesome Howl

A wolf separated from its pack uses a **"lonesome howl"** – a shortened call that rises in pitch. If answered, the wolf responds with deep, even howls to inform the pack of its location.

Who in your life has lost their way and is crying out with a lonesome howl? There are howls we hear with our ears and others we perceive only within our hearts.

"So everyone who acknowledges me before men, I also will acknowledge before my Father who is in heaven."
– Matthew 10:32 ESV

Stamina

Ostriches have tremendous stamina and can maintain speeds up to 38Mph for an hour or more. That means they can run a marathon in about 35 min. A professional cyclist on flat terrain can push for hours at 25mph. In a marathon the ostrich would win every time. In a century (100-mile race) my money would be on the cyclist. Often, we hear that our walk with God is a marathon not a sprint. I believe it is a much longer race, one that requires a lifetime of practice, training and a willingness to put one foot in front of the other.

"Brothers, I do not consider that I have made it my own. But one thing I do: forgetting what lies behind and straining forward to what lies ahead, I press on toward the goal for the prize of the upward call of God in Christ Jesus."
Philippians 3:13-14 ESV

Burden

   This verse has shown up in several of my drawings and paintings this year. I can't tell you how many times I have shifted a heavy burden from one side of my heart to the other, straining to get a full breath from the sheer weight of simply lugging it around. This verse always reminds me that there is a better way. Jesus steps right into our grief, pain, suffering, and troubles. He will, if we allow, take the very burden that is weighing down our heart and replace it with love, acceptance, joy, and a peace that surpasses all understanding. "Come to me, all who labor and are heavy laden, and I will give you rest. Take my yoke upon you, and learn from me, for I am gentle and lowly in heart, and you will find rest for your souls. For my yoke is easy, and my burden is light." Matthew 11:28-30 ESV

Centered

 Green sea turtles are graceful and swift swimmers. They can rest at the bottom of the sea for up to five hours on a single breath and think nothing of migrating thousands of miles each year. But put one on the beach, and it must exert tremendous effort just to wriggle across the sand.

How often do you find yourself struggling in the sand? We end up in these situations because of what we choose to entertain with our eyes, listen to with our ears, or participate in through moral compromise. Lord, help me avoid the temptations that distract and destroy. Help me remain centered in Your current.

"I pray that out of his glorious riches he may strengthen you with power through his Spirit in your inner being," Ephesians 3:16 NIV

Edge of the Universe

In 1929, astronomer Edwin Hubble discovered that galaxies seem to be moving away from each other at speeds proportional to their distance from one another. This relationship, known as Hubble's Law, was the first mathematical evidence that the universe is expanding. The expansion rate is estimated to be about 68 kilometers per second per megaparsec (1 megaparsec = 3.26 million light-years). With our current technology, we can only theorize about the edge of the observable universe, believed to be about 93 billion light-years across (1 light years = 6 trillion miles). Even if you could travel at modern rocket speeds from the edge of the known universe, you would quickly fall behind, as the universe is expanding much faster than any rocket could travel. Cosmologists continue to study the expansion, with some supporting Hubble's calculations while others suggest the universe might be expanding even faster.

Reflection: We are just a tiny speck in the vastness of space, yet this small planet teems with life and precious natural resources. Consider that the very device you're reading this on was made from raw materials extracted from the earth. The deeper I explore science, biology, and mathematics, the more I see how finely tuned and intricately designed the universe is—a testament to the creative hand of God. There are endless wonders to discover, and most certainly, many questions we will never be able to answer. "By faith we understand that the universe was created by the word of God, so that what is seen was not made out of things that are visible." Hebrews 11:3 ESV 139:13-16 ESV

Propitiation

During the days of the Old Testament, sacrifice was a regular occurrence. Often, a lamb or bull was offered as a sin offering – temporary appeasements that needed to be repeated. Jesus represents the full and lasting propitiation. No repeat required.

Propitiation – "averting the wrath of God by the offering of a gift." It refers to turning away God's wrath, the just judgment of our sin, through God's own provision: the sacrifice of Jesus Christ on the cross.

"for all have sinned and fall short of the glory of God, and are justified by his grace as a gift, through the redemption that is in Christ Jesus, whom God put forward as a propitiation by his blood, to be received by faith. This was to show God's righteousness, because in his divine forbearance he had passed over former sins."
Romans 3:23-25 ESV

Humble

Why did Jesus choose a donkey and not a horse for His triumphal entry? Two reasons: a horse at that time symbolized power and was trained for battle, while a donkey represented peace, humility, and was used by the working class to carry heavy loads. This also fulfilled the prophecy from Zachariah 9:9, written 550 years earlier.

"Rejoice greatly, O daughter of Zion! Shout aloud, O daughter of Jerusalem! Behold, your king is coming to you; righteous and having salvation is he, humble and mounted on a donkey, on a colt, the foal of a donkey." Zachariah 9:9 ESV

Whats in a name?

"Rhinoceros" is a Greek word. "Rhino" means "nose" and "ceros" means "horn." Makes sense. But what about the name we are given? Sometimes, a parent simply likes the way a name sounds; other times, it is chosen for its meaning.

The name Jesus is derived from the Hebrew name Yeshua (or Y'shua), meaning "to deliver" or "to rescue." That name carried significant meaning — and an even greater responsibility.

"Because, if you confess with your mouth that Jesus is Lord and believe in your heart that God raised him from the dead, you will be saved. For with the heart, one believes and is justified, and with the mouth one confesses and is saved."
Romans 10:9-10 ESV

Layers

On many occasions, I've found myself making assumptions based solely on a person's external appearance. It brings to mind the timeless wisdom of *"not judging a book by its cover."* When we take the time to truly get to know someone, we uncover the layers that shape their unique personality. This process helps us understand what makes them feel loved and seen, while also allowing us to glimpse the experiences that have left scars.

The verse below reminds me that God sees past the exterior and looks directly at our hearts.

"But the Lord said to Samuel, "Do not look on his appearance or on the height of his stature, because I have rejected him. For the Lord sees not as man sees: man looks on the outward appearance, but the Lord looks on the heart."
1 Samuel 16:7 ESV

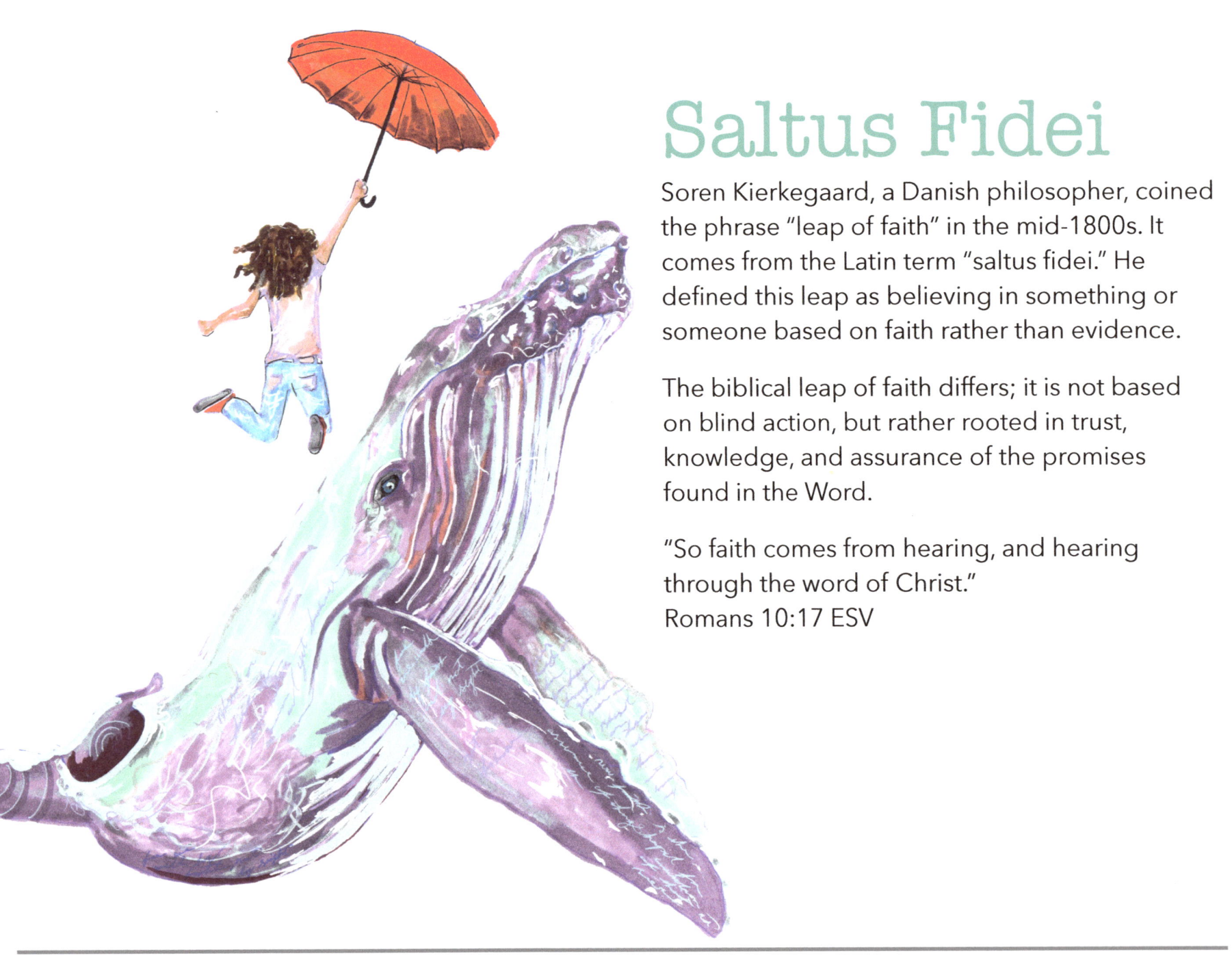

Saltus Fidei

Soren Kierkegaard, a Danish philosopher, coined the phrase "leap of faith" in the mid-1800s. It comes from the Latin term "saltus fidei." He defined this leap as believing in something or someone based on faith rather than evidence.

The biblical leap of faith differs; it is not based on blind action, but rather rooted in trust, knowledge, and assurance of the promises found in the Word.

"So faith comes from hearing, and hearing through the word of Christ."
Romans 10:17 ESV

Watchful

A wolf is always aware of its surroundings. Even while drinking, it keeps its eyes up and ears perked – its survival depends on it. With all the conveniences in our daily lives, it can be tempting to become complacent and let our guard down.

God calls us to be vigilant, prepared, and always ready…

"Be watchful, stand firm in the faith, act like men, be strong. Let all that you do be done in love."
1 Corinthians 16:13-14 ESV

Slug Bug

Driving in winter conditions can be tricky. We go to great lengths to make sure we have the right tires, an AWD vehicle, and even chains. It's unlikely we'd be excited to tackle the Cascade Lakes Highway on a "storm day" in a vintage VW Bug.
At times, we can feel unprepared or lacking the tools to walk the path God has laid before us. Rest assured, God loves to work in and through our weakness. It is when we are weak that others can see His strength shining through us.

"But he said to me, "My grace is sufficient for you, for my power is made perfect in weakness." Therefore I will boast all the more gladly of my weaknesses, so that the power of Christ may rest upon me."
Corinthians 12:9 ESV

Dry Season

Crocodiles like to stay in the same place, but when the dry season comes and the river dries up, they must make a choice. They can either dig into the mud and wait for the rain or pack up and seek a larger body of water.

Some stay encased in mud for up to four months in a semi-hibernation state, while others migrate. Water is essential, as it provides their primary food source — fish — and is key to regulating their body temperature.

We, too, will face dry seasons in life. In those moments, it is crucial for me to remember exactly where my hope comes from. Sometimes I need to dig in, and other times I must move. What remains the same is the source of my hope.

"Jesus said to her, "Everyone who drinks of this water will be thirsty again, but whoever drinks of the water that I will give him will never be thirsty again. The water that I will give him will become in him a spring of water welling up to eternal life."
John 4:13-14 ESV

Lone Wolf

The term "Lone Wolf" stirs up thoughts of a rugged independent individual, driven to forge their own path, ruddy, resourceful and tough as nails. The reality is, a wolf may go through a period of being alone, but they do not thrive in a life of solitude. Wolves prefer to live in packs, they play together into old age, raise their young as a group, hunt collectively, follow well established pack rules, and are known to care for injured companions. The life of a "Lone Wolf" is not just tough, it is borderline impossible. Just like the wolf, we are not meant to do life alone. Today I am thankful for my pack!

"Above all, keep loving one another earnestly, since love covers a multitude of sins. Show hospitality to one another without grumbling. As each has received a gift, use it to serve one another, as good stewards of God's varied grace:"
1 Peter 4:8-10 ESV

Practice

Riding a wheelie on a bike takes loads of practice. I spent a large portion of my childhood trying to perfect the craft. I still find myself riding wheelies and attempting manuals on my mountain bike as an adult.

When we practice something often enough, it becomes almost second nature. Prayer is very similar. If we practice prayer daily, we build spiritual muscle memory and strengthen our relationship with Jesus. Praying daily allows us to be ready when the trail of life gets gnarly.

"pray without ceasing, give thanks in all circumstances; for this is the will of God in Christ Jesus for you."
1 Thessalonians 5:17-18 ESV

The Jeep Wave

If you've spent any time in a Jeep, it doesn't take long to realize that there's a tradition of greeting other Jeep drivers with a wave. The wave dates back to WWII when drivers of the Jeep Willys would greet one another on patrol. After WWII, many servicemen purchased Jeeps, and the tradition continued.

Over time, it has expanded into a broader brotherhood of kindred spirits. Jeep owners share a love for the outdoors, open-air driving, and, some would say, fun over function. I've been a Jeep owner for 27 years, and let me tell you, that quick wave from a fellow Jeepster still puts a smile on my face. It's a reminder that acknowledging one another, even with a simple wave, can be incredibly important.

Challenge: Today, make an effort to say hello to someone you don't know. A small act of kindness can be like a wave in the Jeep world. Who knows, you might just make a new friend or at least brighten someone's day!

"Finally, all of you, be like-minded, be sympathetic, love one another, be compassionate and humble."
1 Peter 3:8 NIV

I worked on this painting over the course of a few weeks. It takes time to add all the layers, and I must be patient, allowing time for the brush strokes to dry before I continue. I can see the end result in my mind, but I can't rush it.

God calls us to exercise patience, for we cannot rush or jump ahead of His plan. Lord, help me to have the patience to wait for the fruit.

"Be patient, therefore, brothers, until the coming of the Lord. See how the farmer waits for the precious fruit of the earth, being patient about it, until it receives the early and the late rains. You also, be patient. Establish your hearts, for the coming of the Lord is at hand."
James 5:7-8 ESV

Patience

Hops

The grasshopper is a marvel of jumping prowess. It can perform a vertical leap 20 times its body length from a complete standstill. Imagine if you had this ability—you could easily leap over a five-story building! But while the jump itself is jaw-dropping, what's even more amazing is its ability to land without a scratch. Scientists and engineers have studied grasshoppers for decades in hopes of unlocking the secrets of their incredible hops. We tend to take movement for granted—until we lose the ability. In Acts 3:6-8, we see a man who most likely thought he'd be sidelined for the rest of his life suddenly jump to his feet in an unbelievable display of strength and healing. Now that's the kind of jump that captures my attention.

"But Peter said, 'I don't have any silver or gold for you. But I'll give you what I have. In the name of Jesus Christ the Nazarene, get up and walk!' Then Peter took the lame man by the right hand and helped him up. And as he did, the man's feet and ankles were instantly healed and strengthened. He jumped up, stood on his feet, and began to walk! Then, walking, leaping, and praising God, he went into the Temple with them." Acts 3:6-8 ESV

Fuel

Have you ever started off on an adventure low on fuel? If you don't feed your body with good, nourishing food, you will lack the energy required to get out of bed, let alone climb a mountain. The same holds true for spiritual nourishment. We must spend time with Jesus if we want to see and participate in what He is doing.

"Abide in me, and I in you. As the branch cannot bear fruit by itself, unless it abides in the vine, neither can you, unless you abide in me."
John 15:4 ESV

Aerobatics

Dragonflies have been closely studied by aerospace engineers for years. Their design is far more complex than any flying machine yet created by man. Their four wings, which can move and rotate independently, allow them to fly up, down, sideways, backward, and even upside down. During a turning maneuver, they generate up to 9Gs of force. For comparison, the typical human will pass out around 4 to 5 Gs.

They have been fondly referred to as mosquito hawks, as they can eat their weight in mosquitoes in just a few hours. When looking at the fossil record, we see that dragonflies are one of the oldest insects. They have shrunk over time but have otherwise remained the same incredible flying machine.

Last fun fact: Dragonflies can carry three times their body weight without affecting their aerobatic capabilities. I stand in awe of this incredible example of the masterful design and creativity of God.

"For his invisible attributes, namely, his eternal power and divine nature, have been clearly perceived, ever since the creation of the world, in the things that have been made. So they are without excuse."
Romans 1:20 ESV

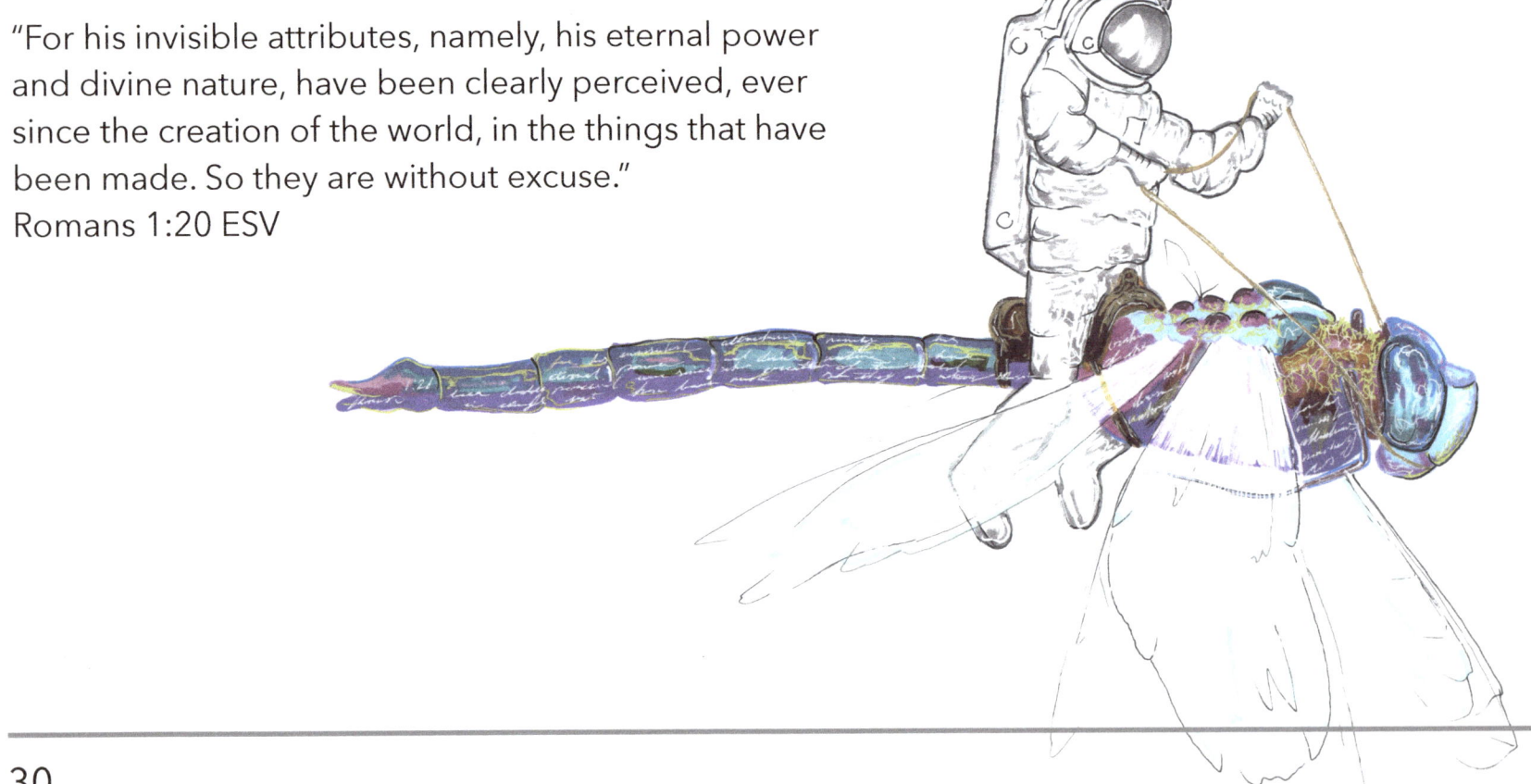

Armor Up

What does it feel like to not only follow but to walk with God? Reading the passage about putting on the armor of God gives us a good indication that it is not a passive act but one that requires trust, preparation, perseverance, and a willingness to risk. This drawing, for me, captures the essence and exuberance of what it feels like to suit up as part of God's team. Just my artistic imagination, as you will not find a rhino riding a cowboy in the Bible.

"Therefore take up the whole armor of God, that you may be able to withstand in the evil day, and having done all, to stand firm. Stand therefore, having fastened on the belt of truth, and having put on the breastplate of righteousness, and, as shoes for your feet, having put on the readiness given by the gospel of peace. In all circumstances take up the shield of faith, with which you can extinguish all the flaming darts of the evil one; and take the helmet of salvation, and the sword of the Spirit, which is the word of God,"
Ephesians 6:13-17 ESV

Nudge

Mother elephants will often nudge their babies to keep them moving in the right direction. Finer directional nudges are given with their trunks, while firmer nudges to move may require a gentle knee to the rear end.

I have experienced many kinds of nudges throughout my life. Some are driven by basic needs—hunger, thirst, fatigue. Some are driven by desires—a shiny new mountain bike, financial security, recognition, or status. Then there are the nudges that make the hairs on my arms stand up. They are typically much more subtle, almost whisper-like, more of a prompting and often easy to miss. This last set is typically associated with helping or meeting the needs of others.

My prayer today: God, help me to pay attention to your quiet whispers. Help me to see others with your eyes, and help me to love others with your heart. And if I still fail to pay attention, feel free to give me a firm but gentle kick in the rear.

"If we live by the Spirit, let us also keep in step with the Spirit." Galatians 5:25 ESV

Mentor

I have had several men in my life over the years who have faithfully spoken truth, provided counsel, loved me through the hard times, and, most importantly, pointed me to Jesus. I am so very thankful for those relationships.

Question: Who in your life has mentored you, and who are you now sowing into?

"Listen, my sons, to a father's instruction; pay attention and gain understanding. I give you sound learning, so do not forsake my teaching. For I too was a son to my father, still tender, and cherished by my mother."
Proverbs 4:1-3 NIV

Tracks

Walking in faith requires trusting God's plan and purpose for our lives—not just when things go our way, but also through life's many storms. At times, it may feel as if we are stepping into the unknown, but rest assured, His tracks will run straight and true.

"In all your ways acknowledge him, and he will make straight your paths."
Proverbs 3:6 ESV

Origin Story

Every year, there are new songs, movies, and books celebrating the legend of Santa Claus. Where did it all start?

It turns out that the real Santa, *St. Nicholas*, was born in the 3rd century AD in Patara (modern-day Turkey). His wealthy parents, who raised him to be a devout Christian, died in an epidemic. Nicholas used his entire inheritance to help the sick, poor, and needy. He was known to keep a low profile, often giving in secret.

One story tells of a poor man with three daughters. In those days, a young woman's father had to offer prospective husbands something of value—a dowry. The larger the dowry, the better the chance that a young woman would find a good husband. Without a dowry, a woman was unlikely to marry. This poor man's daughters, without dowries, were therefore destined to be sold into slavery. Mysteriously, on three different occasions, a bag of gold appeared in their home, providing the needed dowries. The bags of gold, tossed through an open window, are said to have landed in stockings or shoes left before the fire to dry. This led to the custom of children hanging stockings or putting out shoes, eagerly awaiting gifts from Saint Nicholas.

"Each one must give as he has decided in his heart, not reluctantly or under compulsion, for God loves a cheerful giver." 2 Corinthians 9:7 ESV

Waiting

I have been working on this painting during a season of waiting. For me, it represents endurance as we walk through the deserts that appear in our lives. It takes patience, waiting for the rain to come.

"Be patient, therefore, brothers, until the coming of the Lord. See how the farmer waits for the precious fruit of the earth, being patient about it, until it receives the early and the late rains."
James 5:7 ESV

Zero G

In the cosmic dance of "zero G," where gravity supposedly takes a vacation, surprise! Gravity is still an active force. It's like a silent DJ, spinning its beats and constantly drawing you closer.

Picture an astronaut out there, looking like they're floating serenely through space, but guess what? They're actually on a never-ending free fall toward Earth. Zooming at a whopping 17,000 MPH, they're playing cosmic dodgeball, narrowly avoiding a crash thanks to Earth's curved surface. And get this—Isaiah was already dropping hints about this celestial curve back in 700 BC. Talk about an ancient sneak peek!

"It is he who sits above the circle of the earth, and its inhabitants are like grasshoppers; who stretches out the heavens like a curtain, and spreads them like a tent to dwell in;"
Isaiah 40:22 ESV

New Song

Life doesn't always turn out the way we plan. In fact, it rarely does. That said, it never surprises God. When it changes, He already has a new song prepared for you.

"He put a new song in my mouth, a song of praise to our God. Many will see and fear, and put their trust in the Lord."
Psalm 40:3 ESV

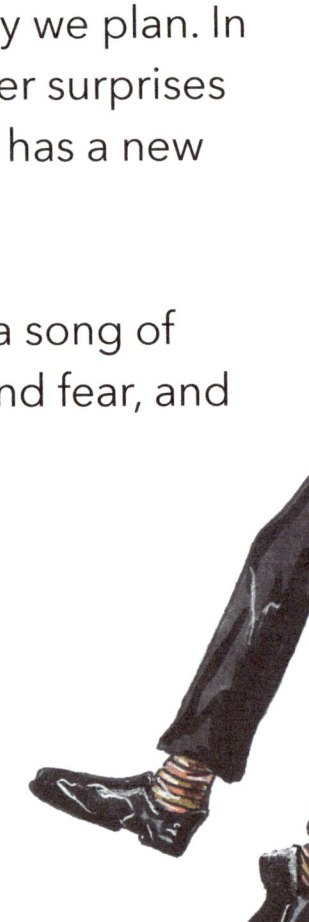

Appearance

Typically, bison are thought of as docile, lumbering creatures, but in reality, a bison can run 30+ mph for four hours straight. Their windpipe and heart are twice the size of those in cattle. Even though a bison can weigh more than a ton, it can jump a six-foot-high fence with a 20-foot running start. And although large, bison can turn or spin on a dime.

We often form opinions based on outward appearance. We are reminded in *1 Samuel* that God sees us differently; He looks beyond our outward appearance and sees our very heart.

"But the Lord said to Samuel, "Do not look on his appearance or on the height of his stature, because I have rejected him. For the Lord sees not as man sees: man looks on the outward appearance, but the Lord looks on the heart."
1 Samuel 16:7 ESV

Trust

Trust – the firm belief in the reliability, truth, or strength of someone or something... Sometimes, faith requires that we step into that trust, balanced only on one wheel. What or how is God asking you to trust Him today?

"Trust in the Lord with all your heart, and do not lean on your own understanding. In all your ways acknowledge him, and he will make straight your paths. Be not wise in your own eyes; fear the Lord, and turn away from evil. It will be healing to your flesh and refreshment to your bones."

Faith

Have you ever seen a cowboy, riding at full speed, rope a steer? If done right, it looks smooth, natural, and almost effortless. I looked up a description of how to use a lasso, but I'll save you pages of reading—this is one task that is very difficult to describe. Some things need to be learned in a hands-on environment. The real "secret sauce" is practice, practice, and more practice.

Stepping out in faith is not something we can learn by reading a description; it can only be experienced when we take that first faith-filled, shaky step and find that our foot has landed on solid ground. Then we take the next step, and the next.

Question: In what way is God asking you to step out in faith?

"for we walk by faith, not by sight."
2 Corinthians 5:7 ESV

Humble

I have found that I can either be humble, or I will eventually be humbled. These are two very different postures. We see a model of living life as a humble servant in Jesus. We get humbled when we are proud, boastful, or when we simply think we are better than others. Jesus, help me take steps to be more like You each day.

"The Lord lifts up the humble; he casts the wicked to the ground."
Psalm 147:6 ESV

Knock

Over the years, I have found that the very things I have attempted to keep hidden in my life are the things I most need God to heal. These are the things that cause shame, embarrassment, regret, and fear. This is not new; we see this same behavior with Adam and Eve hiding from God after they disobeyed. God does not hide from us; He enters into our dark places and patiently waits for us to simply ask for His help and seek His forgiveness.

"Ask and it will be given to you; seek and you will find; knock and the door will be opened to you. For everyone who asks receives; the one who seeks finds; and to the one who knocks, the door will be opened."
Matthew 7:7-8 NIV

Rules

Rules are put in place for a reason. They establish order and prevent us from harming our fellow man. This little sketch is a fun reminder that we are called to abide by those rules, regardless of who we are. Apparently, the Yeti believes that the rule against stealing does not apply to him.

"You know the commandments: 'Do not commit adultery, Do not murder, Do not steal, Do not bear false witness, Honor your father and mother.'"
Luke 18:20 ESV

Motion

Objects in motion tend to stay in motion, and objects at rest tend to stay at rest (Newton). Bicycles are fascinating; they actually rank #1 in efficiency among moving creatures and machines (measured by energy required per gram per kilometer). However, a bike is just yard art without a rider willing to pedal.

In a similar vein, my unread Bible simply gathered dust on a shelf. It wasn't until I cracked it open and spent some quality time with it that I began to see and experience just how deeply God cares for each of us.

"For it is [not your strength, but it is] God who is effectively at work in you, both to will and to work [that is, strengthening, energizing, and creating in you the longing and the ability to fulfill your purpose] for His good pleasure."
Philippians 2:13 AMP

Balancing Act

Life can get a little crazy and, at times, feel like a balancing act. Today, I reflected on what Jesus has taught me about living a full and balanced life:

- *Love others*: This theme is evident throughout his entire ministry.
- *Exercise*: Jesus walked everywhere and often climbed mountains to recharge.
- *Get good rest*: Jesus understood the importance of rest and even power-napped in some interesting places.
- *Seek out and enjoy fellowship*: Throughout scripture, we see Jesus engaging with people from all walks of life—rich and poor, young and old, sick and healthy. He enjoyed fellowship with a diverse range of individuals.
- *Eat well:* Jesus enjoyed a good fish fry, and often broke bread as a way to get to know others.
- *Live a humble life of thanksgiving*: Gratitude was a defining characteristic of his life.
- *Share your hopes, dreams, and burdens with God:* Jesus modeled a disciplined and prayerful life.

Dossan

Highland cows have a long tuft of hair, known as a 'dossan,' that grows down over their eyes. Although it blocks their vision, it does not seem to hinder their ability to find their way. Their thick hair keeps them warm, protects them from pests, and gives them the unique ability to thrive in the harsh Scottish Highland winters. God's creation is truly fascinating.

"For you formed my inward parts; you knitted me together in my mother's womb. It's praise you, for I am fearfully and wonderfully made. Wonderful are your works; my soul knows it very well."
Psalm 139:13-14 ESV

Hang On......

Stepping out in faith and trusting God fully may require us to grab the bars and hang on. Today, I read about Joshua taking on the leadership role after Moses died. Joshua knew that leading the Israelites was too big a task for him to handle on his own. Yet, he chose to move past his fear and put his trust in the Lord. He literally grabbed the bars and hung on for the ride, allowing God to guide him each step of the way.

Lord, help me overcome my fear, apprehension, and doubt. Help me to grab the bars and trust You to lead me each and every step of the way.

> "Have I not commanded you? Be strong and courageous. Do not be frightened, and do not be dismayed, for the Lord your God is with you wherever you go."
> Joshua 1:9 ESV

Training

Being a father is both the hardest and most gratifying part of my life. My boys have taught me to love more deeply than I thought possible. They have made me glow with their antics, laughter, and accomplishments, and they have brought me to my knees and made my blood boil. I am so thankful that they know and trust in Jesus.
Lord, thank You for trusting me to train up my boys.

"Train up a child in the way he should go; even when he is old he will not depart from it." Proverbs 22:6 ESV most important, share your hopes, dreams, and burdens with God. (Jesus demonstrated a disciplined and prayerful life)

Seeds

I find myself in awe of seeds. Without them, the earth would be virtually desolate. To date, we have discovered 280,000 unique seed-bearing plants, trees, shrubs, grasses, and flowers. Most of the food we eat relies on the sprouting, growing, and cultivating of seeds.

I marvel at the fact that the right mix of water, soil, sunlight, and carbon dioxide are the only things required to wake a seed from its dry, crusty, dormant state. Fun fact: the average human exhales about 2.3 pounds of carbon dioxide each day. Plants require carbon dioxide to grow and produce oxygen as a byproduct of photosynthesis, which, in turn, is vital to human existence.

Today, I am thankful for the masterful and creative design of the seed.

"You visit the earth and water it; you greatly enrich it; the river of God is full of water; you provide their grain, for so you have prepared it. You water its furrows abundantly, settling its ridges, softening it with showers, and blessing its growth." Psalm 65:9-10 ESV

Journey

Mount Rainier towers 14,410 feet above sea level. Climbers face a challenging vertical elevation gain of 9,000 feet over a distance of 8 miles to reach the summit. Less talked about is the 93-mile Wonderland Trail that circles the mountain, taking you through glacier valleys, subalpine meadows, temperate rainforests, and a volcanic ridge. Often, we focus on tackling a problem head-on—climbing straight up—but many times, God is asking us to do more than solve a problem. He wants to take us on a journey that not only solves the problem but also changes our hearts.

"And I will give you a new heart, and a new spirit I will put within you. And I will remove the heart of stone from your flesh and give you a heart of flesh. And I will put my Spirit within you, and cause you to walk in my statutes and be careful to obey my rules." Ezekiel 36:26-27 ESV

Wonder

Children innately have a strong sense of wonder and a high propensity to imagine. Wonder has a tendency to atrophy as we age. Our minds get bound up with daily responsibilities, tasks, and obligations. We simply take less time to question, imagine, and wonder.

Thought to ponder - despite modern technology, only 5% of the oceans have been explored (primarily at surface level). 95% remain untouched and unseen. Space - our universe is vast and continuously expanding. Astronomers collectively understand roughly 5%. Pause for a moment today to stop and simply wonder at the beauty and intricacy that surrounds you.

"The heavens declare the glory of God, and the sky above proclaims his handiwork. Day to day pours out speech, and night to night reveals knowledge."
Psalm 19:1-2 ESV

Distraction

Distraction: The average person spends 3+ hours a day staring into their pocket-sized portal. Today's challenge: put your phone down and take note of the big and small things; ponder the fact that we live in a fully functioning closed system. Every drop of water we see has been here from the beginning. In the PNW, some of the very water we surf during the summer will cycle from the ocean to cloud vapor, to the high mountain snow we ride on during the winter. It then melts and flows from streams to rivers, and back to the ocean once again.

The water cycle is actually much more complex and fascinating, providing a renewable and clean source for crops, consumption, and play. A clean glass of water drawn from a well is a gift—and absolutely incredible, considering just how many times it may have been through the cycle.

"Do not be conformed to this world, but be transformed by the renewal of your mind, that by testing you may discern what is the will of God, what is good and acceptable and perfect." Romans 12:2 ESV

Lonesome Howl

Feels like winter. Previously, when I first sketched out the wolf, I wrote about the lonesome howl. I thought about it a lot as I worked on this painting. It is the howl a wolf, separated from its pack, uses to seek help in finding its way back. There are howls that we hear with our ears and others that we only perceive within our hearts. At times, we may lack the strength to whisper, let alone cry out for help.

Lord, help us to hear within our souls the inner howls of those who have lost their way and are seeking help to find their way home to You.

"Ask, and it will be given to you; seek, and you will find; knock, and it will be opened to you. For everyone who asks receives, and the one who seeks finds, and to the one who knocks it will be opened."
Matthew 7:7-8 ESV

Only 0.7%

71% of the earth's surface is covered by water. Of that, 96.5% is salt water contained within the oceans. 3.5% of the water on earth is fresh, but 69% of that exists in the form of ice found in the polar ice fields. Only 0.7% exists in the form of lakes, streams, rivers, groundwater, and cloud vapor. Scientists once thought that our planet began its existence as dry, molten mass, with water showing up millions of years later. However, more recent research conducted by the Woods Hole Oceanographic Institution (WHOI) in Woods Hole, Massachusetts, points to water appearing in earth's earliest days.

Our planet is a fascinating example of a fully functioning closed system. The natural resources available are astounding. They provide the essentials for life, as well as the raw materials to build cities, vehicles, and supercomputers. From a resource perspective, we want for nothing.

"He set the earth on its foundations, so that it should never be moved. You covered it with the deep as with a garment; the waters stood above the mountains. At your rebuke they fled; at the sound of your thunder they took to flight. The mountains rose, the valleys sank down to the place that you appointed for them. You set a boundary that they may not pass, so that they might not again cover the earth. You make springs gush forth in the valleys; they flow between the hills; they give drink to every beast of the field; the wild donkeys quench their thirst. Beside them the birds of the heavens dwell; they sing among the branches. From your lofty abode you water the mountains; the earth is satisfied with the fruit of your work." Psalm 104:5-13 ESV

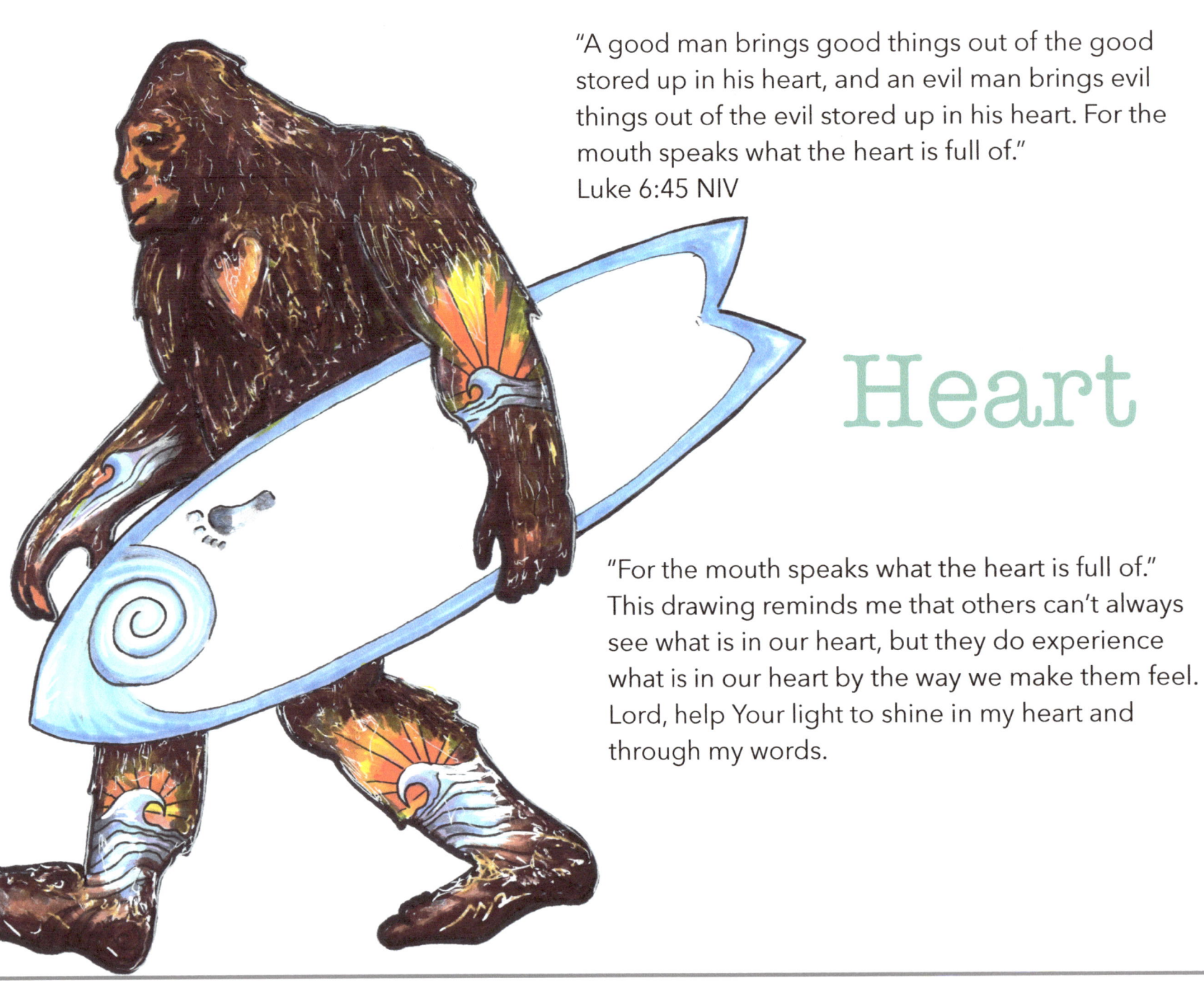

"A good man brings good things out of the good stored up in his heart, and an evil man brings evil things out of the evil stored up in his heart. For the mouth speaks what the heart is full of."
Luke 6:45 NIV

Heart

"For the mouth speaks what the heart is full of." This drawing reminds me that others can't always see what is in our heart, but they do experience what is in our heart by the way we make them feel. Lord, help Your light to shine in my heart and through my words.

Rain Down

Have you ever wondered if you are seen by God? Have you ever questioned if He has heard you crying out? I can tell you, without a shadow of a doubt, that He sees and hears you. He knows every painful moment, and He can tell you about each tear. He not only walks with us through the storm, but He also carries us when we lack the strength to carry on.

"You keep track of all my sorrows. You have collected all my tears in your bottle. You have recorded each one in your book."
Psalms 56:8 NLT

Lion and Lamb

When John the Baptist was about to baptize Jesus, he described Him as the Lamb of God who takes away the sins of the world (John 1:29). We associate characteristics with a lamb, such as gentleness, tenderness, and even submissiveness (John 5:19).

While Jesus embodies all of these qualities, there is another side to Him. He is also described in the Bible as the Lion of Judah—noble, honorable, capable, worthy, and never backing down from evil.

Is Jesus a Lion or a Lamb?   The answer is a definitive yes to both. (Revelation 5:5-6)

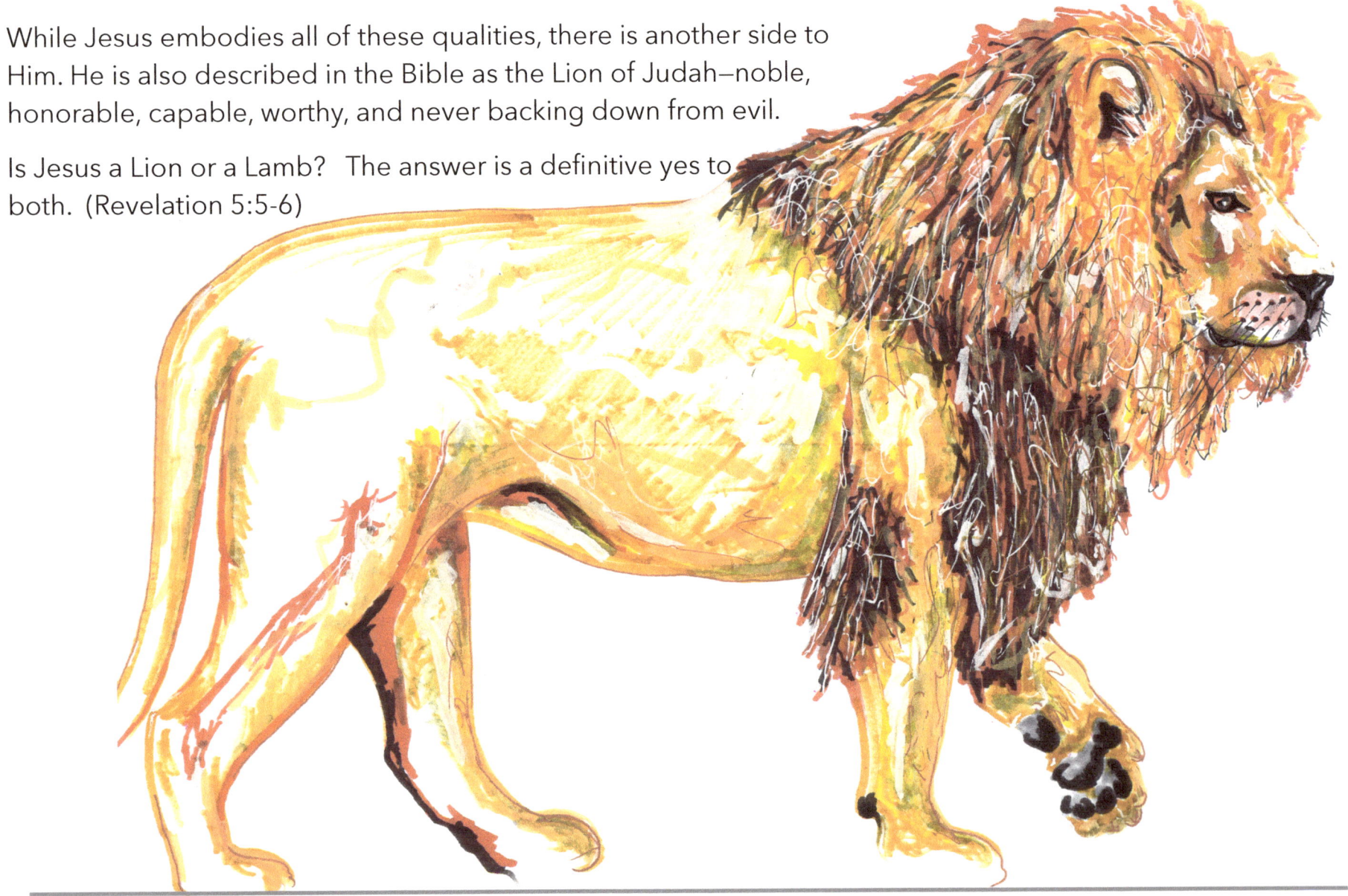

What Comes Next

We spend most of our lives thinking that the "next" is something earthly—meeting a goal, getting that perfect job, buying a car, etc. But what comes next-next? Fifty-four of the sixty-six books in the Bible have verses about Heaven. Jesus mentions Heaven seventy times in the book of Matthew alone. We don't have to wonder what's next… Heaven is the ultimate "next" that will last for eternity.

"For we know that when this earthly tent we live in is taken down (that is, when we die and leave this earthly body), we will have a house in heaven, an eternal body made for us by God himself and not by human hands."
2 Corinthians 5:1 NLT

Helpmate

1,056,475,286—that's the number of seconds I have known my wife, Lynda. Of those, 23,678,600 were spent in Paris, France—the inspiration for this drawing. And yes, we did dance in the streets a few times!

We met our freshman year of college and have walked side by side through the highest of highs and the lowest of lows. As I sketched this piece, I reflected on the years and couldn't imagine a better helpmate to navigate this crazy world with.

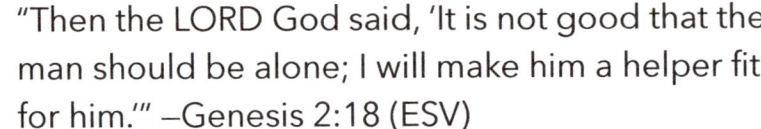

"Then the LORD God said, 'It is not good that the man should be alone; I will make him a helper fit for him.'" —Genesis 2:18 (ESV)

Scripture often compares our relationship with God to a marriage. And if there's one thing I've learned, it's that without effort from both sides—shared goals, values, and constant investment—marriage won't flourish. The same is true for our relationship with God. If we neglect time, energy, and intentionality, He may seem distant—a far-off, nebulous being. But the reality is, He deeply desires a relationship with each of us.

James 4:8 ESV reminds us: "Draw near to God, and He will draw near to you."

Challenge: Put in a little extra effort to draw near to God. For me, it has been the best investment I have ever made. And as for my helpmate, I am eternally grateful for the wife God has graced me with.

What Comes Next

We spend most of our lives thinking that the "next" is something earthly—meeting a goal, getting that perfect job, buying a car, etc. But what comes next-next? Fifty-four of the sixty-six books in the Bible have verses about Heaven. Jesus mentions Heaven seventy times in the book of Matthew alone. We don't have to wonder what's next… Heaven is the ultimate "next" that will last for eternity.

"For we know that when this earthly tent we live in is taken down (that is, when we die and leave this earthly body), we will have a house in heaven, an eternal body made for us by God himself and not by human hands."
2 Corinthians 5:1 NLT

Helpmate

1,056,475,286—that's the number of seconds I have known my wife, Lynda. Of those, 23,678,600 were spent in Paris, France—the inspiration for this drawing. And yes, we did dance in the streets a few times!

We met our freshman year of college and have walked side by side through the highest of highs and the lowest of lows. As I sketched this piece, I reflected on the years and couldn't imagine a better helpmate to navigate this crazy world with.

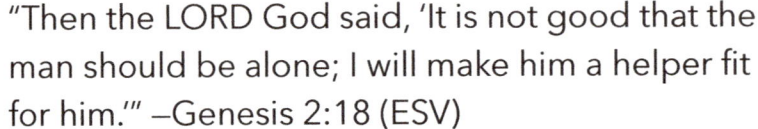

"Then the LORD God said, 'It is not good that the man should be alone; I will make him a helper fit for him.'" –Genesis 2:18 (ESV)

Scripture often compares our relationship with God to a marriage. And if there's one thing I've learned, it's that without effort from both sides—shared goals, values, and constant investment—marriage won't flourish. The same is true for our relationship with God. If we neglect time, energy, and intentionality, He may seem distant—a far-off, nebulous being. But the reality is, He deeply desires a relationship with each of us.

James 4:8 ESV reminds us: "Draw near to God, and He will draw near to you."

Challenge: Put in a little extra effort to draw near to God. For me, it has been the best investment I have ever made. And as for my helpmate, I am eternally grateful for the wife God has graced me with.

"There is no fear in love, but perfect love casts out fear. For fear has to do with punishment, and whoever fears has not been perfected in love." 1 John 4:18 ESV

Cubes

I have been working on this painting off and on for a few months. I am loosely following the method of cubism. As I have been painting, I have reflected on all of the attributes, traits, beliefs, experiences, and relationships that have shaped me as a person. Each cube/rectangle represents a small piece of that. Some of them I have attempted to hide, while others I have worn at times like a badge of honor. Ultimately, the bits and pieces come together to form the image I present to others.

During this time of reflection, it has become more apparent than ever that God loves us deeply. Nothing is hidden from Him; He sees it all and still pours out His love unrestricted.

Better Together

How often have you found yourself in a situation where a friend has been there just at the right time to lift you up, encourage you, lend a hand, or simply listen? We are designed for community, and we are better together. Today, I find myself being grateful for all of the amazing people God has put into my life.

Question to ponder: Who is God asking you to encourage today?

"Two are better than one, because they have a good reward for their toil. For if they fall, one will lift up his fellow. But woe to him who is alone when he falls and has not another to lift him up!" Ecclesiastes 4:9-10 ESV

Outside of Time!

Time, as I know it, is a precious commodity. It is the one thing I cannot get more of! It is the very currency I must trade for anything I decide to do—work, play, sleep, eat, love, laugh, fight, etc. It all costs time.

God does not exist within this same constraint. He is outside of our timeline. He sees the entire picture; there are no surprises, and He never grows weary. He does not worry and he does not suffer from anxiety. Creating the universe was simple for Him—one could almost compare it to a leisurely cruise through the park.

Psalm 90:4 (ESV): "For a thousand years in your sight are but as yesterday when it is past, or as a watch in the night."

Imagine being outside of time, seeing creation, events, and life as a complete tapestry rather than in fragments. Such a thought causes my mind to do mental gymnastics, yet it results in nothing but more questions. For now, I will continue to explore the moments—one at a time.

"He has made everything beautiful in its time. He has also set eternity in the human heart; yet no one can fathom what God has done from beginning to end." Ecclesiastes 3:11 NIV

Faith is a Gift

You may have heard the term "God-given gift," or, put another way, "Wowzers, that kid is a natural!" A gift can be used for God, used selfishly, or even wasted altogether. Paul reminds us that faith is a gift, and like anything else we want to grow in, it requires attention, practice, and time.

"I am reminded of your sincere faith, a faith that dwelt first in your grandmother Lois and your mother Eunice and now, I am sure, dwells in you as well. For this reason, I remind you to fan into flame the gift of God, which is in you through the laying on of my hands, for God gave us a spirit not of fear but of power and love and self-control."
2 Timothy 1:5-7 ESV

Commitment

We just spent four days surfing on the Oregon coast, so I still have waves on my brain. Surfing requires patience and is an exercise in interpreting tides, currents, geography, swell, shape, energy, and timing. Knowing which waves are good comes only with time, practice, experience, and a keen Spidey-sense. The final ingredient is commitment! This means turning, paddling, and allowing your board and body to drop down the face of the wave. Any hesitation, and you've missed it.

Following the Lord takes a similar mindset. We must be patient, watch what He is doing, and be prepared to drop in. We must demonstrate full commitment and trust. When we experience failure, we take a breath and paddle back out.

Lord, help me to be all in. Help me to wait on what You are doing. Help me to not get distracted, discouraged, or waste energy on fruitless pursuits.

"Wait for the Lord; be strong, and let your heart take courage; wait for the Lord!"
Psalm 27:14 ESV

Big and Small

If you assume a grain of sand has an average size, calculate how many grains fit in a teaspoon, and then multiply that by all the beaches and deserts in the world, the Earth has roughly (and we're speaking very roughly here) 7.5×10^{18} grains of sand—or seven quintillion, five hundred quadrillion grains. That number is unimaginably large. However, the grains of sand do not outnumber the stars in the heavens. It is estimated that there are 200 sextillion stars (200,000,000,000,000,000,000,000). That number is so vast, it's hard to comprehend. But try this: it's about 10 times the number of cups of water in all the oceans on Earth. This may all feel overwhelmingly immense, but here's a fun fact: you'll find the same number of molecules in just ten drops of water!

Today, I find myself thankful that God is present in both the big and the small things. I am captivated by His attention to detail and humbled that He not only knows every grain of sand and every star in the sky but also knows and cares for me.

"You saw me before I was born. Every day of my life was recorded in your book. Every moment was laid out before a single day had passed. How precious are your thoughts about me, O God. They cannot be numbered! I can't even count them; they outnumber the grains of sand! And when I wake up, you are still with me!"   Psalms 139:16-18 NLT

Be Still

Have you ever found yourself in a tough spot and wondered where God is? Sometimes, we're simply not looking in the right place. God is constantly moving on our behalf, but we can't always feel or see it.

In Psalm 46, God reminds us to "Be still, and know that I am God." In Psalm 27:14, we find encouragement: "Wait for the Lord; be strong, and let your heart take courage; wait for the Lord!" In Jeremiah 29, we are promised that He hears us.

"For I know the plans I have for you, declares the Lord, plans for welfare and not for evil, to give you a future and a hope. Then you will call upon me and come and pray to me, and I will hear you. You will seek me and find me, when you seek me with all your heart."
Jeremiah 29:11-13 ESV

Value

Feathers Worth More Than Gold?
In the early 1900s, feather collectors nearly eradicated the Great Egret. The shoulder-length plumes, called aigrettes, were wildly popular in hats and sold for $30 an ounce—twice the price of gold at the turn of the century. Fortunately for the birds, the hats eventually went out of vogue.

God knows you personally and values you far beyond your comprehension! In Psalm 56, David alludes to the fact that God not only knows our suffering but also takes note of and accounts for every tear we shed:
"You have kept count of my tossings; put my tears in your bottle. Are they not in your book?" Psalm 56:8 ESV

Man may value feathers and gold, but God values us, even to the point of storing our very tears.

Thankful

Stop! Take a deep breath and pause for a moment. Acknowledge all that you have to be thankful for: the air you breathe, the food in your pantry, the people in your life, the wildlife, and the array of plants, flowers, and trees. I stand in awe and wonder at the beauty, diversity, and vastness of God's creation.

"Every good gift and every perfect gift is from above, coming down from the Father of lights with whom there is no variation or shadow due to change."
James 1:17 ESV

Sure-Footed

Llamas have padded feet with a split toe! This quirky design gives them superhero-level traction. Pair that with their ability to use their head and neck for counterbalance, and you've got the ultimate mountain-climbing buddy. Forget four-wheel drive—these guys are all about four-foot finesse!

But wait, there's more! Llamas have oval-shaped red blood cells, which is like having turbocharged oxygen power. This nifty feature lets them thrive at dizzying elevation of up to 16,000 feet. Pretty cool, right?

So, why all this talk about fancy feet and supercharged lungs? Well, life can sometimes feel like you're teetering on the edge, ready to slip. We get anxious about the past and nervous about what's ahead. Here's the deal: the bad news is, tough times are guaranteed. The good news? God never intended for us to face them alone.

I'm so grateful for His unfailing love, encouraging Word—and for the gift of balance, split toes and all.

Psalm 94:18-19
"When I said, "My foot is slipping," your unfailing love, Lord, supported me. When anxiety was great within me, your consolation brought me joy."

Trust

When you find yourself in a bind, who or what do you turn to for help? I often find myself running in circles, doing my best to fix the problem on my own, yet gaining little to no ground. God wants us to know that we can trust Him in both the big and the small—in our everyday lives and most certainly in our times of crisis.

Lord, help me to trust You in all that I do.

"I lift up my eyes to the hills. From where does my help come? My help comes from the Lord, who made heaven and earth. He will not let your foot be moved; he who keeps you will not slumber."
Psalm 121:1-3 ESV

The 72

Who were the 72? We don't have specifics. We know that Jesus sent them out two by two to spread the word. He told them to be wary of danger, live by faith, stay focused, be content, and bless those they encountered. I imagine they traveled with urgency and a great sense of purpose.

"After this the Lord appointed seventy-two others and sent them on ahead of him, two by two, into every town and place where he himself was about to go. And he said to them, "The harvest is plentiful, but the laborers are few. Therefore pray earnestly to the Lord of the harvest to send out laborers into his harvest. Go your way; behold, I am sending you out as lambs in the midst of wolves."
Luke 10:1-3 ESV

Trust

When you find yourself in a bind, who or what do you turn to for help? I often find myself running in circles, doing my best to fix the problem on my own, yet gaining little to no ground. God wants us to know that we can trust Him in both the big and the small—in our everyday lives and most certainly in our times of crisis.

Lord, help me to trust You in all that I do.

"I lift up my eyes to the hills. From where does my help come? My help comes from the Lord, who made heaven and earth. He will not let your foot be moved; he who keeps you will not slumber."
Psalm 121:1-3 ESV

The 72

Who were the 72? We don't have specifics. We know that Jesus sent them out two by two to spread the word. He told them to be wary of danger, live by faith, stay focused, be content, and bless those they encountered. I imagine they traveled with urgency and a great sense of purpose.

"After this the Lord appointed seventy-two others and sent them on ahead of him, two by two, into every town and place where he himself was about to go. And he said to them, "The harvest is plentiful, but the laborers are few. Therefore pray earnestly to the Lord of the harvest to send out laborers into his harvest. Go your way; behold, I am sending you out as lambs in the midst of wolves."
Luke 10:1-3 ESV

Sing

Thinking about my goals this morning. Some are small, and some feel huge, but they pale in comparison to the God-sized goals we find in the Bible. Imagine, for a moment, getting the whole earth to sing unto the Lord.

"Oh sing to the Lord a new song; sing to the Lord, all the earth!"
Psalm 96:1 ESV

Better Together

Both the male and female eagle share in the care, feeding, protection, and training up of their young. God created them to work together, each taking on very important roles. They need each other to succeed. God created us to work together.

"Though one may be overpowered, two can defend themselves. A cord of three strands is not quickly broken."
Ecclesiastes 4:12 NIV

Extraordinary

Jesus asked four fishermen to stop what they were doing and follow Him. These were ordinary, hard-working gents, not scholars. Jesus loves to take the ordinary and make it extraordinary.

"While walking by the Sea of Galilee, he saw two brothers, Simon (who is called Peter) and Andrew his brother, casting a net into the sea, for they were fishermen. And he said to them, "Follow me, and I will make you fishers of men." Immediately they left their nets and followed him. And going on from there he saw two other brothers, James the son of Zebedee and John his brother, in the boat with Zebedee their father, mending their nets, and he called them. Immediately they left the boat and their father and followed him."
Matthew 4:18-22 ESV

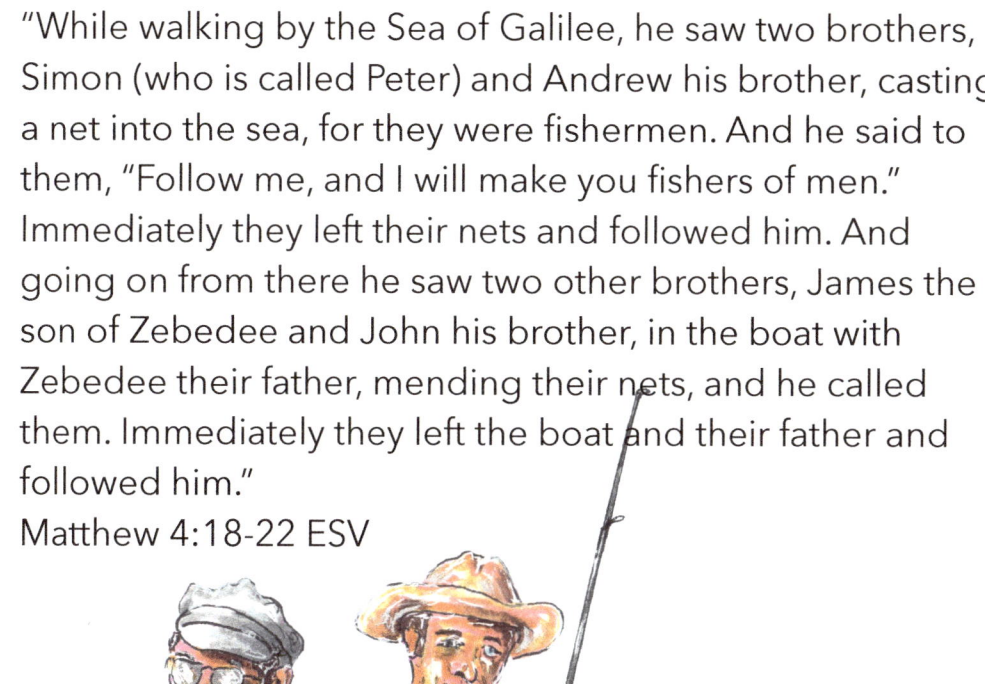

Polar Plunge

Polar bears are the ultimate Arctic residents, hanging out in the frosty wilds of Alaska, Canada, Russia, Greenland, and Norway. They're basically built for the cold, rocking thick, hollow fur, a cozy blubber layer, and webbing between their toes, perfect for land-and-sea action. These powerhouses think nothing of -50° F temperatures and routinely dive into the super chilled waters to snag dinner. Talk about cool confidence—literally.

This drawing, titled *Polar Plunge,* got me thinking: we're all equipped with our own kind of "polar bear gear"—unique gifts and talents from God. The question is, how are we using them to serve others? And are we brave enough to take a plunge outside our comfort zone?

The rule of the Polar Plunge says, "If you don't get your head wet, it doesn't count." Take a chance today, step outside your comfort zone, bring a bit of hope into someone's day.

"I can do all things through him who strengthens me."
Philippians 4:13 ESV

"As each has received a gift, use it to serve one another, as good stewards of God's varied grace."
1 Peter 4:10 ESV

The Potter

God knows you; He sees you, and He is deeply in love with you (His creation). It is amazing to think that we are like clay in God's hands. He can work and rework us, shaping each of us for a unique purpose. And when we lose focus, crash, and burn, God scoops us back up and shapes us again.

Jeremiah 18:1-6 ESV The word that came to Jeremiah from the Lord: "Arise, and go down to the potter's house, and there I will let you hear my words." So I went down to the potter's house, and there he was working at his wheel. And the vessel he was making of clay was spoiled in the potter's hand, and he reworked it into another vessel, as it seemed good to the potter to do. Then the word of the Lord came to me: "O house of Israel, can I not do with you as this potter has done?" declares the Lord. Behold, like the clay in the potter's hand, so are you in my hand, O house of Israel."

Patience

Demonstrating and practicing patience is not my strong suit. I am the "get it done" sort of guy. God has been teaching me that, in order to walk with Him, I must be willing to wait, be still, and keep my mind free from distractions so I can listen.

"Wait for the Lord; be strong, and let your heart take courage; wait for the Lord!"
Psalm 27:14 ESV

Time

Time is a treasured currency that we trade for the things we need, want, and desire. I need shelter, so I trade time at work for money to pay for the roof over my head. I trade time to seek fresh powder turns, to draw and paint, and I traded time to write and illustrate this book. I have often taken time for granted or simply wasted or squandered it. Many times, I have procrastinated, putting this or that off until tomorrow, next week, or next year. Jesus reminds us that action may be required sooner than we think. Sharing the hope you have with others may not happen if you put it off. Who in your life needs to know just how much God loves them?

"Don't you have a saying, 'It's still four months until harvest'? I tell you, open your eyes and look at the fields! They are ripe for harvest."
John 4:35 NIV

"Wait for the Lord; be strong, and let your heart take courage; wait for the Lord!"
Psalm 27:14 ESV

Faith like a Tuna

Bluefin tunas have been known to weigh as much as 1,500 pounds and measure 12 feet from nose to tail. Although they are well known as one of the largest fish, they begin life no more than a few millimeters long. Within a few years, they reach 3 feet and continue to grow for as long as 35 years. Faith typically begins as a small spark and grows over time. Often, we hear the term "faith like a mustard seed," as a very large plant is produced from a very small seed.

"He said to them, "Because of your little faith. For truly, I say to you, if you have faith like a grain of mustard seed, you will say to this mountain, 'Move from here to there,' and it will move, and nothing will be impossible for you."
Mathew 17:20 ESV

Storm Worthy

Archimedes is responsible for explaining why a boat floats in water—the net upward force on an object immersed in water is equal to the weight of the water displaced by the object.

[(mass of boat + mass of cargo) * (0.01 Newtons / g)] - [(mass of displaced water) * (0.01 N / g)]

This discovery was a breakthrough that significantly advanced watercraft design. While buoyancy is essential for any seaworthy vessel, it's not the only factor. A boat must be thoughtfully designed, rigorously tested, and properly equipped for the journey ahead. Thinking about this made me reflect on my own faith journey. Just as a boat needs to be watertight to withstand storms, our faith needs a solid foundation. Self-reflection is vital—asking ourselves if we're holding onto any "baggage" that might cause us to sink. Life's storms will come, often unexpectedly, and when they do, we don't want to be stuck in a leaky boat without a paddle.

"God is our refuge and strength, a very present help in trouble. Therefore we will not fear though the earth gives way, though the mountains be moved into the heart of the sea, though its waters roar and foam, though the mountains tremble at its swelling. Selah" Psalm 46:1-3 ESV

Reflection

Our hearts will reveal and reflect who we truly are. A friend of mine challenged me to strive to be more like Jesus each day. I like this challenge and am attempting to put it into practice, but I realize there will be days when I fail miserably. I am so very thankful that it is by grace we are saved. I am also grateful that this grace is offered as a free gift to all, regardless of how well we may have measured up today or in the past.

"As in water face reflects face, so the heart of man reflects the man."
Proverbs 27:19 ESV

"For by grace you have been saved through faith. And this is not your own doing; it is the gift of God,"
Ephesians 2:8 ESV

Flip the Script

When we read the story of Jonah, we find a reluctant prophet—a man with previous grievances who doesn't want to do what God is asking. Long story short, after running from God, Jonah finds himself in the belly of a whale—dark, alone, and regretting his decision (Jonah chapters 1 and 2).

Imagine, for a moment, if Jonah had immediately said "yes." Rather than being vomited up on the shores of Nineveh, maybe he could have ridden there triumphantly on the back of the same whale. This is just how my artist's imagination works, but how often are we reluctant, or simply ignore God's prompting altogether? Lord, help me say "yes" to Your plan the first time, and help me to trust You each and every step of the way.

Fathers

My father believed in leading by example. Growing up, my dad was the hardest-working man I knew, yet he still found time to take me fishing, teach me to shoot, pull me for hours on my wakeboard behind the boat, and, of course, help me build a solid work ethic. I am thankful for the father God provided me, and I am grateful that he always encouraged me to give my best.

"And he will turn the hearts of fathers to their children and the hearts of children to their fathers, lest I come and strike the land with a decree of utter destruction." Malachi 4:6 ESV

Current

Green sea turtles are graceful and swift swimmers. They can rest at the bottom of the sea for up to five hours on a single breath, and think nothing of migrating a few thousand miles each year. Put one on the beach, and it must exert tremendous effort to simply wriggle across the sand. How often do you find yourself struggling in the sand? We put ourselves into these situations based on what we choose to entertain with our eyes, listen to with our ears, or participate in through moral compromise.
Lord, help me to avoid the temptations that distract and destroy. Help me to remain centered in Your current.

"I pray that out of his glorious riches he may strengthen you with power through his Spirit in your inner being,"
Ephesians 3:16 NIV

Pressure

I grew up in Ellensburg, Washington, one of the windiest towns in the state. Nestled just east of the Cascades, it's essentially kite-flying heaven. Why? It all comes down to pressure. On the west side, cool, coastal high-pressure air pushes up against the Cascades. On the east side, warm, low-pressure, sun-kissed air lingers. When that cooler, denser air spills through a gap in the mountains called the Stampede Gap, it creates a breeze that funnels straight into Ellensburg.

It got me thinking: life is a bit like that wind. Every day, we face all kinds of pressures. We can't help but spill out what's stored up in our hearts and minds. The way we move through the world can either lift people up or leave them feeling knocked around. Lord, help me be the kind of breeze that refreshes, encourages, and renews—bringing Your peace wherever I go.

"For God has not destined us for wrath, but to obtain salvation through our Lord Jesus Christ, who died for us so that whether we are awake or asleep we might live with him. Therefore encourage one another and build one another up, just as you are doing."
1 Thessalonians 5:9-11 ESV

Wonders

I try to do a whimsical drawing every Wednesday. Today I was inspired by Psalms 65:8

"Those who live at the ends of the earth stand in awe of your wonders. From where the sun rises to where it sets, you inspire shouts of joy."
Psalms 65:8 NLT

Faith like a Child

If you want to see true faith mixed with a healthy dose of determination, watch a toddler learning to walk. As we grow older, we become much more self-conscious and may even shy away from things that are uncertain, challenging, or simply put us in a position of looking foolish. Faith like a child means stepping out on wobbly legs with the expectation that you will eventually be able to run. Lord, help me to have faith like a child.

"But when Jesus saw it, he was indignant and said to them, "Let the children come to me; do not hinder them, for to such belongs the kingdom of God. Truly, I say to you, whoever does not receive the kingdom of God like a child shall not enter it."" Mark 10:14-15 ESV

Sing

Male humpback whales love to sing. Their songs can last up to 20 minutes and may be repeated for hours. All the males within a geographic area (spanning up to 3,000 miles) sing the same song, which gradually changes each year. Scientists suspect the songs are used for communication, location, and even fellowship. While we may never fully understand the nuances of their songs, we can see the amazing Creator in His creation.

"Let everything that has breath praise the Lord! Praise the Lord!"
Psalm 150:6 ESV

God's Current

Ocean currents are the invisible highways of the sea, the behind-the-scenes magic that allows sea turtles to pull off epic migrations spanning thousands of miles. These aquatic superhighways let turtles hop in, go with the flow, and enjoy the ride.

Reflection: Walking in faith means stepping into God's current, trusting the speed He's set, believing His timing is spot-on, and resisting the urge to grumble about detours or pit stops along the way. Sounds easy, right? Spoiler alert: it's not. This is a journey that will span a lifetime. There will be moments when it feels like you're swimming against the current, struggling to move an inch. But here's the good news—God's patience is deeper than any ocean. He's the Captain of second chances... and third, fourth, fifth, and however many it takes to get you back on course. So, grab your snorkel, trust the Captain, and dive in!

"For we walk by faith, not by sight."
2 Corinthians 5:7 ESV

"Commit to the Lord whatever you do, and he will establish your plans." - Proverbs 16:3 ESV

Love Bears All

I recently completed a painting called *Love Bears All Things*. It reminds me that we could have the whole world, but without love, we would still feel empty. Jesus told us that the two most important commandments are: 1) love God above all else, and 2) love our neighbors. I have written the following verse into the painting at least a dozen times: "Love bears all things, believes all things, hopes all things, endures all things."
—1 Corinthians 13:7 (ESV)

Experiential Learning

Experiential learning is the process of learning by doing. In childhood, this type of hands-on learning comes almost naturally. We observe and try things with little thought given to failure or the potential embarrassment of looking awkward. I am grateful for the amazing mentors I have had over the years, especially those who took the extra time to teach experientially. I am also thankful for the childlike awe and wonder I experience through the exploration of my faith.

"But as for you, continue in what you have learned and have firmly believed, knowing from whom you learned it and how from childhood you have been acquainted with the sacred writings, which are able to make you wise for salvation through faith in Christ Jesus." 2 Timothy 3:14-15 ESV

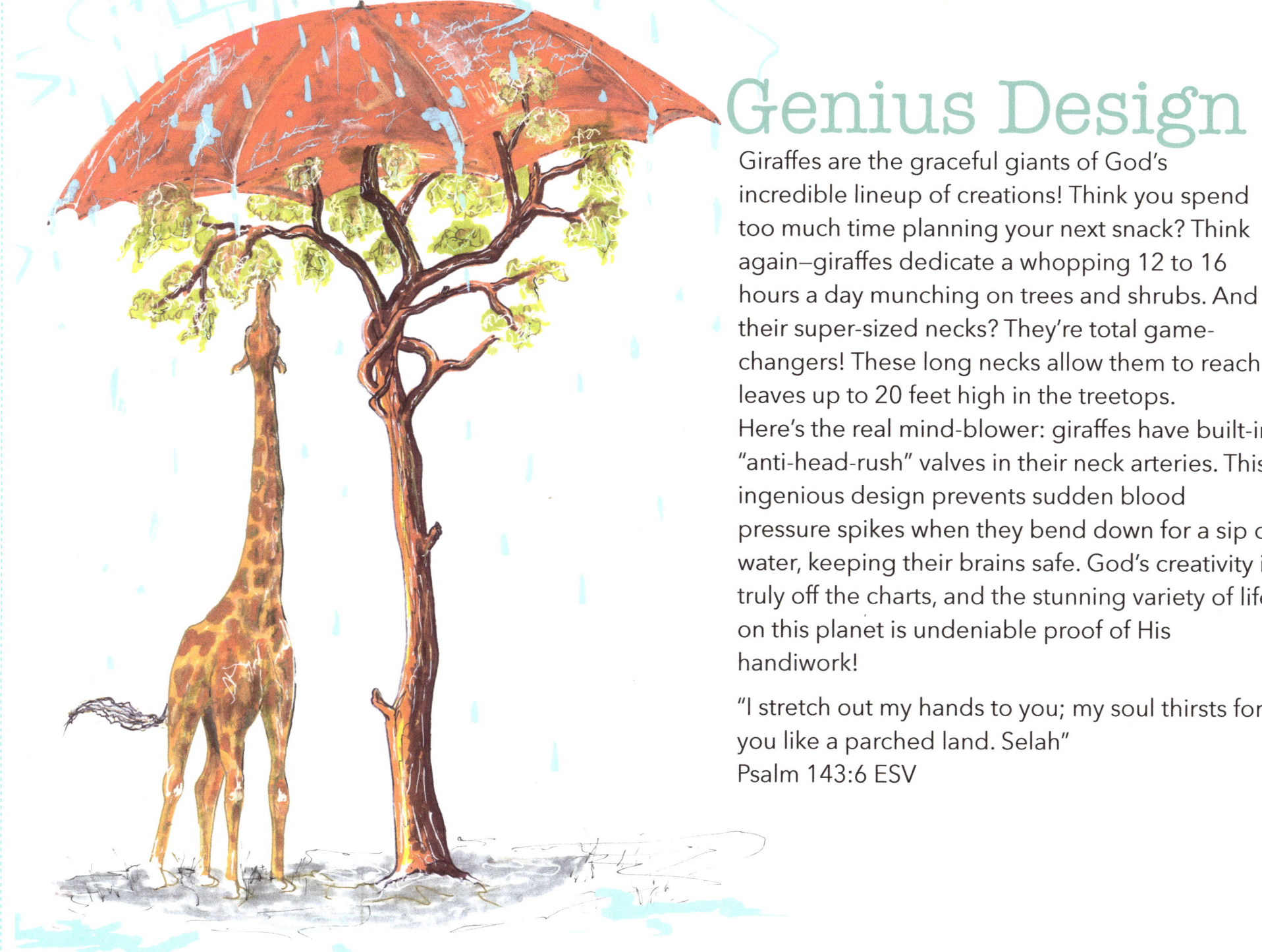

Genius Design

Giraffes are the graceful giants of God's incredible lineup of creations! Think you spend too much time planning your next snack? Think again—giraffes dedicate a whopping 12 to 16 hours a day munching on trees and shrubs. And their super-sized necks? They're total game-changers! These long necks allow them to reach leaves up to 20 feet high in the treetops.

Here's the real mind-blower: giraffes have built-in "anti-head-rush" valves in their neck arteries. This ingenious design prevents sudden blood pressure spikes when they bend down for a sip of water, keeping their brains safe. God's creativity is truly off the charts, and the stunning variety of life on this planet is undeniable proof of His handiwork!

"I stretch out my hands to you; my soul thirsts for you like a parched land. Selah"
Psalm 143:6 ESV

Scrubbing

The Green Sea Turtle has a pretty cool nickname: the ocean's lawnmower. Why? Because it trims seagrass meadows like a pro, keeping them neat and healthy. But while they're munching away, algae can start to pile up on their shells and flippers—like unwanted hitchhikers—making them itchy and slow. So, what's a turtle to do? Head to a reef-side spa, of course! These "cleaning stations" are hangouts where hardworking surgeonfish nibble off the clingy algae, giving the turtles a much-needed scrub. Once the spa session is over, the turtles glide away squeaky clean, feeling fresh and ready for their next big swim.

Question: What part of your life could use a good scrub and a fresh start?

"Wash yourselves; make yourselves clean; remove the evil of your deeds from before my eyes; cease to do evil, learn to do good; seek justice, correct oppression; bring justice to the fatherless, plead the widow's cause."
Isaiah 1:16-17 ESV

You reflect what you consume

Why are flamingos pink?
Flamingos' feathers, which are naturally a dirty white color, gradually turn pink from eating vegetation rich in carotenoids—a substance that gives blue-green algae its reddish hue. If their diet changes, their feathers will fade back to white.

Similarly, spending time with God allows His attributes to shine in and through our daily lives. Galatians outlines a few:

"But the fruit of the Spirit is love, joy, peace, patience, kindness, goodness, faithfulness, gentleness, self-control; against such things there is no law."
Galatians 5:22-23 ESV

Training up

Mother elephants are incredibly loyal, fiercely protective, and meticulously attentive. Their pregnancies last for two years, and the average elephant baby weighs a whopping 200 pounds. These dedicated mothers take the responsibility of teaching and training very seriously, working tirelessly to prepare their offspring for adulthood.

Challenge: Think about someone who has taken the time to invest in you. Let them know how thankful you are!

"Hear, my son, your father's instruction, and forsake not your mother's teaching, for they are a graceful garland for your head and pendants for your neck. My son, if sinners entice you, do not consent."
Proverbs 1:8-10 ESV

You reflect what you consume

Why are flamingos pink?

Flamingos' feathers, which are naturally a dirty white color, gradually turn pink from eating vegetation rich in carotenoids—a substance that gives blue-green algae its reddish hue. If their diet changes, their feathers will fade back to white.

Similarly, spending time with God allows His attributes to shine in and through our daily lives. Galatians outlines a few:

"But the fruit of the Spirit is love, joy, peace, patience, kindness, goodness, faithfulness, gentleness, self-control; against such things there is no law."
Galatians 5:22-23 ESV

Training up

Mother elephants are incredibly loyal, fiercely protective, and meticulously attentive. Their pregnancies last for two years, and the average elephant baby weighs a whopping 200 pounds. These dedicated mothers take the responsibility of teaching and training very seriously, working tirelessly to prepare their offspring for adulthood.

Challenge: Think about someone who has taken the time to invest in you. Let them know how thankful you are!

"Hear, my son, your father's instruction, and forsake not your mother's teaching, for they are a graceful garland for your head and pendants for your neck. My son, if sinners entice you, do not consent."
Proverbs 1:8-10 ESV

Flicker

Zacchaeus was a chief tax collector—a position that made him very wealthy but also caused him to be disliked and seen as untrustworthy by the people. He had heard that Jesus was traveling through and wanted to catch a glimpse of Him. Being short in stature and unable to see over the crowd, Zacchaeus ran ahead and climbed a sycamore tree.

When Jesus passed by, He stopped, looked up, and told Zacchaeus to come down, as He wanted to join him for dinner. The people grumbled, seeing Zacchaeus as unworthy. However, Zacchaeus immediately came down and repented, promising to pay back four times the amount to anyone he had cheated.

Reading this story, I realized that Jesus sees us so differently than we see ourselves. He sees our potential and knows what we are capable of. He recognizes the light of God shining within us and helps even the smallest flicker grow into a burning flame.

"Jesus responded, "Salvation has come to this home today, for this man has shown himself to be a true son of Abraham. For the Son of Man came to seek and save those who are lost.""
Luke 19:9-10 NLT

Words

Words have the power to build up and the power to destroy. Lord, help me control my words; help me speak life, truth, and compassion.

"People can tame all kinds of animals, birds, reptiles, and fish, but no one can tame the tongue. It is restless and evil, full of deadly poison. Sometimes it praises our Lord and Father, and sometimes it curses those who have been made in the image of God. And so blessing and cursing come pouring out of the same mouth. Surely, my brothers and sisters, this is not right! Does a spring of water bubble out with both fresh water and bitter water?"
James 3:7-11 NLT

Step onto His Train

What journey is God preparing you for? In my walk with God, I have embarked on many unexpected adventures. More often than not, these experiences have given me a fresh appreciation for life and a deeper love for others. I often don't know where He is leading me next, but I have come to realize that if I want to walk with Him, I must be willing to step aboard His train.

"And he said to them, "The harvest is plentiful, but the laborers are few. Therefore pray earnestly to the Lord of the harvest to send out laborers into his harvest."
Luke 10:2 ESV

Reflecting

I'm fascinated by the fact that polar bear fur isn't actually white. A few months ago, I learned it's translucent, and the white color we see is simply light being reflected. Similarly, we reflect what we give our attention to—how we spend our time and the things we read, listen to, and watch.

It makes me wonder: What am I reflecting today? And what do I want to reflect tomorrow?

"Search me, O God, and know my heart! Try me and know my thoughts! And see if there be any grievous way in me, and lead me in the way everlasting!"
Psalm 139:23-24 ESV

Leap

Manta rays are among the largest fish, with a wingspan of up to 21 feet. Silent and graceful, these filter-feeding swimmers glide effortlessly through the ocean. Unlike other rays equipped with barbed stingers, manta rays are stingerless and completely harmless to humans. Occasionally, they can be seen leaping out of the water, momentarily appearing to fly above the surface. Scientists speculate that this behavior may serve as communication, a mating ritual, or a way to rid themselves of parasites, but the exact reason remains a mystery.

I take a simpler view: I believe they leap out of the water for the same reason we jump in. We were created to play and explore as we move through this world.

"Now the Lord is the Spirit, and where the Spirit of the Lord is, there is freedom."
2 Corinthians 3:17 ESV

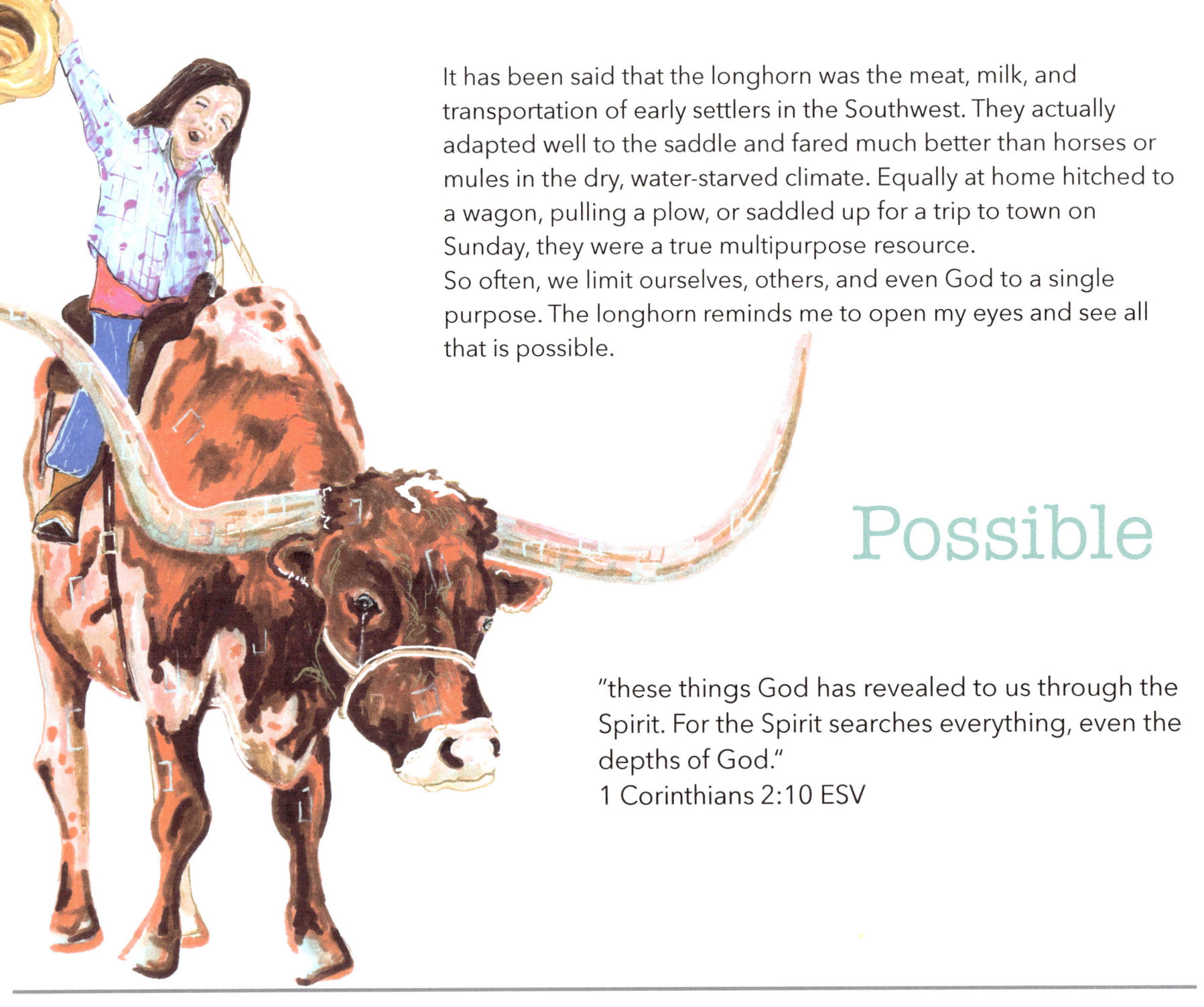

It has been said that the longhorn was the meat, milk, and transportation of early settlers in the Southwest. They actually adapted well to the saddle and fared much better than horses or mules in the dry, water-starved climate. Equally at home hitched to a wagon, pulling a plow, or saddled up for a trip to town on Sunday, they were a true multipurpose resource.

So often, we limit ourselves, others, and even God to a single purpose. The longhorn reminds me to open my eyes and see all that is possible.

Possible

"these things God has revealed to us through the Spirit. For the Spirit searches everything, even the depths of God."
1 Corinthians 2:10 ESV

Elephants Can't Jump!

Elephants likely don't give much thought to jumping, especially since they possess one of the most extraordinary appendages among mammals—their trunk. Devoid of joints or bones, this muscular multi-tool can uproot trees, serve as a snorkel during river crossings, provide a shower, lift objects with precise vacuum suction, and even sniff out and pluck the perfect banana.

Elephants aren't amazed by the versatility of their trunks; they simply use the incredible tool God gave them to navigate their world. Thinking about our own hands and feet, I can't help but marvel at the creativity of our Designer.

"But ask the animals, and they will teach you, or the birds in the sky, and they will tell you; or speak to the earth, and it will teach you, or let the fish in the sea inform you. Which of all these does not know that the hand of the Lord has done this? In his hand is the life of every creature and the breath of all mankind." Job 12:7-10 ESV

Gator holes

Alligators tend to get a bad rap, but they are actually classified as a keystone species. This means they have a significant impact on their ecosystem. If they were to disappear, swamps would change dramatically. Gators dig "gator holes," essentially creating wetlands within wetlands. These gator holes retain water even during the driest spells, providing habitat for fish, turtles, and wading birds.
We often face problems, adversity, and trials. In those times, life can feel dry, empty, and even hopeless. Yet God shows up in the unlikeliest of places and points us to a "gator hole," where we can rest, recover, and emerge with renewed faith, hope, and love.

"Not only so, but we also glory in our sufferings, because we know that suffering produces perseverance; perseverance, character; and character, hope."
Romans 5:3-4 NIV

First Impressions

The Wawona Tunnel was completed in April 1933. At 4,233 feet in length, it holds the record as the longest tunnel in the State of California. Drilled through solid granite, the portal leads Yosemite visitors from the South Entrance to an awe-inspiring, jaw-dropping view of Yosemite Valley, showcasing icons such as El Capitan, Bridalveil Falls, and Half Dome. Photos, drawings, and paintings can only capture the essence of this magnificent view. My first impression was pure awe. Yet this view, despite its grandeur, is merely an appetizer for the wonders that await us in Heaven..

For what can be known about God is plain to them, because God has shown it to them. For his invisible attributes, namely, his eternal power and divine nature, have been clearly perceived, ever since the creation of the world, in the things that have been made. So, they are without excuse. Romans 1:19-20 ESV

Tunnel View
First Impressions

Signs

While in Yosemite, we saw numerous signs warning that bears frequented the area and shared the trails. The signs were so common that I eventually stopped noticing them. I didn't fully appreciate their significance until we spotted a bear while hiking back from the Mist Trail. In that moment, the signs took on a whole new meaning. It made me reflect on how often I get distracted and possibly miss important reminders that are right in front of me.

"Therefore I intend always to remind you of these qualities, though you know them and are established in the truth that you have." 2 Peter 1:12 ESV

"For this very reason, make every effort to supplement your faith with virtue, and virtue with knowledge, and knowledge with self-control, and self-control with steadfastness, and steadfastness with godliness, and godliness with brotherly affection, and brotherly affection with love." 2 Peter 1:5-7 ESV

DEJA QUE TU LUZ BRILLE

The Vermilion Rockfish is found in rocky reefs off the Northern Pacific Coast where there are plenty of large boulders and outcrops to hide. They thrive in cool waters at depths from 50'- 300', but have been observed as deep as 900'. Although brightly colored, they spend most of their time hidden. Their vivid color is only observed when they are brought into the light. I found myself thinking about how often I elect to remain hidden among the rocks. Being vulnerable with others can feel uncomfortable and risky. Today I am reminded to - Deja que tu luz brille (Let your light shine)

"You are the light of the world. A city set on a hill cannot be hidden. Nor do people light a lamp and put it under a basket, but on a stand, and it gives light to all in the house. In the same way, let your light shine before others, so that they may see your good works and give glory to your Father who is in heaven."
Matthew 5:14-16 ESV

Imagination

As an artist, I am grateful for the gift of imagination—the act of forming a mental image of something not present to the senses or never before wholly perceived in reality. Imagination is just a sliver of the secret sauce that makes us human. Our mind is a precious gift. It holds the keys to our personality, allows us to exercise creativity, solve problems, and enables us to give and receive love. As I write this, I am reminded that our minds are heavily influenced by the things we allow in. Said another way, we reflect the things we choose to consume.

"You keep him in perfect peace whose mind is stayed on you, because he trusts in you."
Isaiah 26:3 ESV

"Do not be conformed to this world, but be transformed by the renewal of your mind, that by testing you may discern what is the will of God, what is good and acceptable and perfect."
Romans 12:2 ESV

Intention

During a recent trip along the Oregon Coast, I found myself pondering: just how salty is the ocean? On average, there's 35 grams of salt per kilogram of seawater. This balance remains constant because each year, the amount of salt naturally added through mineral erosion (from rain to streams to rivers to oceans) is roughly offset by losses due to evaporation and settling. Maintaining this equilibrium in ocean salinity is crucial for marine life, ocean currents, and even the buoyancy of polar ice sheets. Any significant deviation could trigger profound global repercussions. It's moments like these that remind me of the intricacies and precision woven into our planet's design.

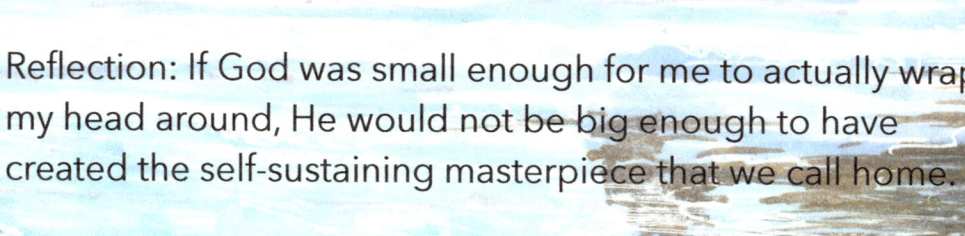

Reflection: If God was small enough for me to actually wrap my head around, He would not be big enough to have created the self-sustaining masterpiece that we call home.

"For my thoughts are not your thoughts, neither are your ways my ways, declares the Lord. For as the heavens are higher than the earth, so are my ways higher than your ways and my thoughts than your thoughts." Isaiah 55:8-9 ESV

Gravity

In physics, gravity (from Latin *gravitas*, meaning 'weight') is a fundamental interaction that causes mutual attraction between all things that have mass. Objects with more mass exert more gravitational force. Gravity also weakens with distance, so the closer objects are to each other, the stronger their gravitational pull. Gravity is what keeps our feet firmly planted on the ground. The Moon, being one-sixth the size of Earth, has only one-sixth the gravity. Less gravity means some fascinating things can happen! On the Moon, you would experience a slippery sensation, almost like walking on ice, and your vertical jump—averaging 9.8 feet—would make you feel superhuman. Surfing in low gravity would be an entirely new adventure.

Reflection – Gravity is an invisible yet very powerful force. You cannot physically see it, but you can observe its effects whenever objects are in motion. Similarly, faith, though invisible, is a powerful force that has transformed the way I see, react, and navigate through life. Faith provides hope and assurance of something much bigger than myself. The closer I draw to my Creator, the stronger His "gravitational pull" becomes, influencing every aspect of my life.

"And he is before all things, and in him all things hold together."
Colossians 1:17 ESV

"By faith we understand that the universe was created by the word of God, so that what is seen was not made out of things that are visible."
Hebrews 11:3 ESV

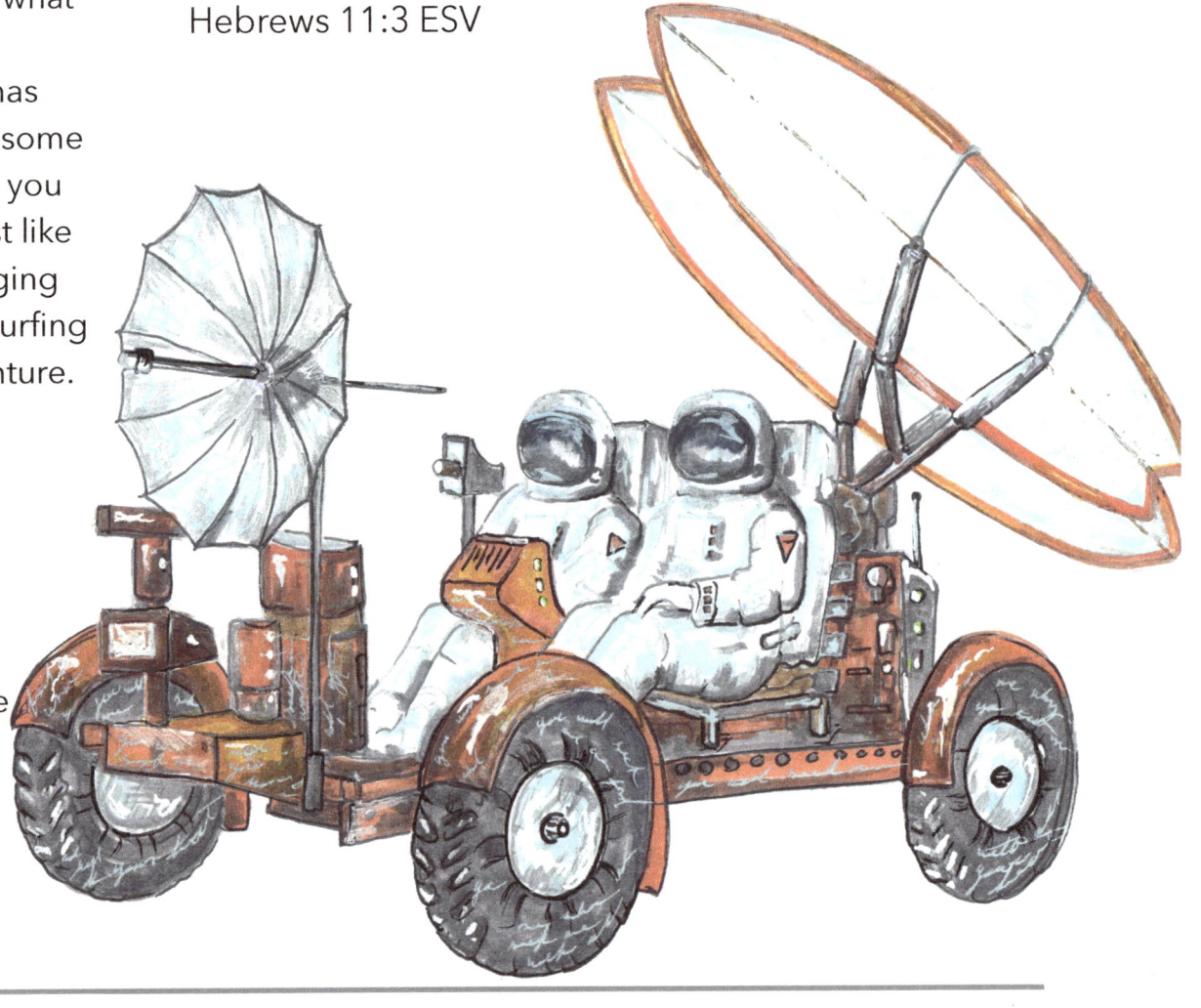

Thoughts and lines captured in my journal from a rainy morning at Stimulus Coffee… A double espresso, an inquisitive dog on the beach, and a verse in Isaiah sparked some reflections that led my mind to dive into the mathematical gymnastics of probability….

Isaiah wrote the following passage 700 years before Christ would be crucified. "But he was pierced for our transgressions; he was crushed for our iniquities; upon him was the chastisement that brought us peace, and with his wounds we are healed." Isaiah 53:5 ESV In total, Jesus fulfilled more than 300 prophecies.

Mathematician Peter W. Stoner calculated that the probability of one man in all of history fulfilling just eight of the prophecies found in the Old Testament would be 10^{17}, or 1 in 100,000,000,000,000,000. That is an astronomically large number. The odds of fulfilling forty-eight prophecies would be 10^{157}—a figure with 157 zeros.

Random or by design? The math strongly points to the latter.

Probability!

Cosmic balancing act

A few weeks ago, I wrote about gravity—the fundamental interaction that causes mutual attraction between all things with mass. A fun side effect of the gravitational pull generated between the Earth, Moon, and Sun is ocean tides. As a sometimes surfer, I spend a fair amount of time checking forecasts and tide charts. The tide, working in conjunction with a favorable swell, is the secret sauce for a great session.

Question: If the Moon and Earth are pulling toward one another, what keeps them from crashing into each other?

Answer: Movement. The Earth spins at 733 miles per hour and moves through its orbit around the Sun at 67,000 miles per hour. The Moon orbits the Earth at 2,288 miles per hour. Gravitational pull, spin, and orbit work together in a masterfully designed cosmic balancing act, allowing us to feel stable, observe cycles, experience seasons, and, yes, count on high tides being 12 hours and 25 minutes apart each day.

"And he is before all things, and in him all things hold together."
Colossians 1:17 ESV

Metamorphosis

Monarchs, like other butterflies and moths, undergo complete metamorphosis, meaning they have an egg, larva (caterpillar), pupa (chrysalis), and adult stage. Adult Monarch butterflies live, on average, for 2 to 5 weeks. This means that in the spring and summer, we see three generations of Monarchs. Something very different happens in the fall. The fourth generation of butterflies emerges, bulks up on nectar, clusters together, and begins a long migration south to Central Mexico—a place that neither their parents nor grandparents have seen. This generation lives through the winter, and in early spring, migrates north, where they lay eggs that will become the season's first generation.

Reflection: Metamorphosis is a complete transformation; a slow, squishy caterpillar that may have lived its life on a single milkweed plant emerges as a butterfly capable of flying thousands of miles. I found myself asking the question: What does a transformed heart look like? What does it look like to step out in faith, to dig deeper, and to go farther than those who have come before you? What does it look like to have a fourth-generation heart?

"I will sprinkle clean water on you, and you shall be clean from all your uncleannesses, and from all your idols I will cleanse you. And I will give you a new heart, and a new spirit I will put within you. And I will remove the heart of stone from your flesh and give you a heart of flesh." Ezekiel 36:25-26 ESV

Surfer or Sleigh-boy

St. Nicholas – A Surfer or a Sleigh-Boy?

St. Nicholas was born around 280 A.D. in Patara, a beach town near Myra in modern-day Turkey. An only child, he tragically lost his affluent parents during an epidemic.

A devoted follower of Jesus, Nicholas felt compelled to serve others. He used his inheritance to assist the needy, care for the sick, comfort the suffering, and was especially known for his generosity toward children.

The story of St. Nicholas is one of tragedy turned into purpose—an orphan determined to give back and a man devoted to faithfully serving others.

To answer the initial question: given his proximity to and love for the sea, he was far more likely to be a surfer than a sleigh-boy.

"You will be enriched in every way to be generous in every way, which through us will produce thanksgiving to God."
2 Corinthians 9:11 ESV

Mighty Protector

Not the first thing that comes to mind when looking at an ostrich, is it? Best known for their incredible running ability, ostriches are also highly skilled at defending themselves with their powerful legs. They can deliver devastating kicks with a force of up to 2,000 pounds per square inch. When combined with their sharp, 4-inch talons, ostriches have even been known to go head-to-head with lions.

Why "mighty protector"? Ostriches are dedicated parents, teaching and fiercely protecting their young until they are fully grown.

Reflection: While writing this, I thought of my own mighty protector. I am deeply grateful that His protection does not stop at adulthood. On the contrary, it is eternal. It does not end when this life does; it has no expiration and is a promise that will never be broken.

"The Lord is your keeper; the Lord is your shade on your right hand. The sun shall not strike you by day, nor the moon by night. The Lord will keep you from all evil; he will keep your life. The Lord will keep your going out and your coming in from this time forth and forevermore." Psalm 121:5-8 ESV

"Peacocking"

Today, I was thinking about appearances—we are currently visiting Banff National Park. Each trail we hike brings us not only a deep appreciation of God's amazing creation but also close proximity to people from all over the world. Most are dressed in some sort of outdoor garb, enjoying the beauty of the park, but some have taken their "fit" to the extreme to capture Instagram-worthy selfies.

This reminded me of the term *peacocking*—a social behavior in which an individual uses ostentatious clothing and actions to stand out from others, aiming to be more memorable and interesting.

Reflection: Jesus, arguably the most memorable person to have walked this earth, was the polar opposite of "peacocking." Jesus exhibited compassion (*Matthew 9:36*), served others (*Mark 10:45*), forgave freely (*Luke 23:34*), and embodied love, commitment, prayerfulness, gentleness, patience, self-control, and humility.

Marks & Scars

Grey whales, ancient travelers of the deep,
Grace the oceans with a journey bold and steep—
Five thousand miles from Alaskan cold to Mexico's warm, sunlit fold.
From afar, they seem like shadows in the sea,
Smooth and grey, moving silently.
But up close, their skin tells a different tale,
Marked with patterns like ink on sail.

This unique patterning begins just after birth from barnacles and whale lice, and becomes more distinct into adulthood through deeper scarring received when defending the young and weaker members of the pod from Orcas.

-And so, too, in life, the storms will rise,
Leaving scars both distinct and faint.
But unshaken, a truth stands clear—
We never walk alone in our fear.
I know this well: when darkness prevails,
God is there, in every gale.
He not only walks beside your strife—
He carries you through the fiercest days of life.

"When you pass through the waters, I will be with you; and through the rivers, they shall not overwhelm you; when you walk through fire you shall not be burned, and the flame shall not consume you." Isaiah 43:2 ESV

Balance in motion

Gravity is the invisible force that keeps the Moon in its 2,288 MPH orbit around the Earth, the Earth in its 67,000 MPH orbit around the Sun, and the Sun pulling all the planets along at 450,000 MPH as it orbits the center of the Milky Way Galaxy. But it doesn't stop there—the Milky Way Galaxy is also in motion. Astronomers continue to discover larger systems of celestial bodies in even larger orbits.

Reflection: Space—pull the thread, and it ignites a sense of awe and wonder. It provides a peekaboo glimpse into God's creative and intelligent design and demonstrates the perfection observed through "balance in motion."

"The heavens declare the glory of God, and the sky above proclaims his handiwork. Day to day pours out speech, and night to night reveals knowledge." Psalm 19:1-2 ESV

Dive deep

Polar bear fur isn't actually white—it's translucent with a hollow core. This unique fur provides critical insulation and excellent camouflage. On snowy tundra, it appears bright white; in shadows, it looks gray; and in water, it can take on a slight bluish tint. The fur reflects light, allowing polar bears to blend almost seamlessly into the Arctic environment.

In addition to being strong swimmers, some polar bears have been observed diving to great depths, holding their breath for up to three minutes while hunting for food. They develop this skill gradually, starting with playful dives as cubs and perfecting it over time through practice.

Reflection: The light we reflect to others mirrors what we take in through our eyes, ears, and hearts. Sometimes, life requires us to dive deep, drawing on our inner reserves. In those moments, we will reflect exactly what we've practiced daily and stored within our heart and mind.

"Finally, brothers, whatever is true, whatever is honorable, whatever is just, whatever is pure, whatever is lovely, whatever is commendable, if there is any excellence, if there is anything worthy of praise, think about these things. What you have learned and received and heard and seen in me practice these things, and the God of peace will be with you."
Philippians 4:8-9 ESV

"You keep him in perfect peace whose mind is stayed on you, because he trusts in you."
Isaiah 26:3 ESV

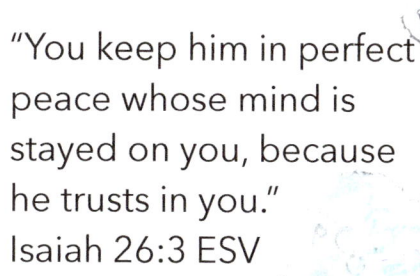

Shake off the distractions Of this World

Although all penguins are exceptional swimmers, the Gentoo would claim the gold medal in a sprint race. These incredible swimmers can reach speeds of up to 35 km/h in the water. Gentoo penguins are known to "porpoise" through the water, leaping in and out to increase their speed. They also jump into the air before diving, releasing air bubbles from their feathers to enhance hydrodynamics for smoother, faster swimming.

Their speed and agility not only make them excellent fishermen but also protect them from the larger dangers that lurk just below the surface.

Reflection: Before jumping in and diving deep, it's important to take time to prepare—shake off distractions and rid ourselves of the day-to-day debris that weighs us down. Only then can we fully embrace the magnitude of the plan God is asking us to take part in.

"Therefore, since we are surrounded by so great a cloud of witnesses, let us also lay aside every weight, and sin which clings so closely, and let us run with endurance the race that is set before us," Hebrews 12:1

Perspective

In 2011, scientists observed a polar bear in the Beaufort Sea swim non-stop for nine days, covering an astonishing 426 miles of open water before finally reaching land. To put that into perspective, standing on a beach on a clear day, you can only see about 2.8 miles out to sea. Due to the curvature of the Earth, everything beyond the horizon fades out of view. This means the polar bear completed 98.7% of its swim completely out of sight from land.

Reflection: Our perspective greatly influences how we see things. At sea level, our view is limited to 2.8 miles. If we climb 100 feet above the beach, the horizon stretches to 12.8 miles. From 5,000 feet, we can see as far as 93.5 miles. A typical Starlink satellite, orbiting 340 miles above Earth, has an enormous field of view and circles the globe every 90 minutes. In what areas are you viewing a problem from sea level that could look very different from higher ground? Conversely, in what areas, like the polar bear, do you simply need to keep swimming, trusting that solid ground is within reach—even if you cannot yet see it?

"Hear my cry, O God, listen to my prayer; from the end of the earth I call to you when my heart is faint. Lead me to the rock that is higher than I, for you have been my refuge, a strong tower against the enemy." Psalm 61:1-3 ESV

"For this light momentary affliction is preparing for us an eternal weight of glory beyond all comparison, as we look not to the things that are seen but to the things that are unseen. For the things that are seen are transient, but the things that are unseen are eternal." 2 Corinthians 4:17-18 ESV

Every Eye

As an artist, I find the Bible to be full of pen to paper, thought provoking inspiration. Reading Revelation 1:7, I imagine in my mind what Jesus coming in a cloud would look like (of course, with creative license exercised). "Behold, he is coming with the clouds, and every eye will see him, even those who pierced him, and all tribes of the earth will wail on account of him. Even so. Amen."
Revelation 1:7 ESV

When I read Revelation 3:8, I realize that Jesus is the door that cannot be shut.

He is a refuge that cannot be stolen, a promise that cannot be broken, and a truth that is perfect without flaw. I am so very thankful that He accepts me right where I am—earnestly trying, yet still broken, flawed, and weak.

"Behold, I have set before you an open door, which no one is able to shut. I know that you have but little power, and yet you have kept my word and have not denied my name." Revelation 3:8 ESV

Watching the rain over the last few days, I couldn't help but wonder: just how much rain falls in a year? If you were to take the total rainfall across the globe and spread it evenly, every region would get about 39 inches rain annually. But of course, that's not how it works! For example, Arica, Chile, only gets about 0.02 inches of rain a year, while Mawsynram, India, gets a mind-blowing 467 inches. Now here's a fun fact: every single minute, 264 billion gallons of water fall on Earth! That's enough to fill 400,000 Olympic-sized pools. According to NASA, about 500,000 cubic kilometers of rain fall worldwide each year. And here's the coolest part—no new water is added to make that happen. Our planet's water system is a genius, closed-loop cycle that constantly cleans and recycles water. So next time it rains, think about this: how many times has that drop of water fallen before?

Rain drops

"As the rain and the snow come down from heaven, and do not return to it without watering the earth and making it bud and flourish, so that it yields seed the sower and bread for the eater, so is my word that goes out from my mouth: It will not return to me empty, but will accomplish what I desire and achieve the purpose for which sent it."
Isaiah 55:10-11 NIV

One of my favorite Old Testament books is Daniel. It is a great reminder that not much has changed in the last few thousand years. Politicians and leaders of the day dug up dirt and slung mud to get ahead, people lied and cheated, and fear was often used as a motivator. It is also the origin of the commonly used phrases "the writing is on the wall" and "walking through the fire."

Daniel was an impressive man, demonstrating unshakable faith, character, and resolve. Taken captive as a young teen and brought to a foreign land, he showed great promise, was educated, and rose through the ranks, serving five kings during his life. He was 86 years old when he found himself facing execution due to a targeted edict stating that anyone who bowed to any god or man other than the current king, Darius, would be thrown to the lions. Daniel did not waver or hide his faith; he continued to pray three times per day, as was his custom. The king saw Daniel as one of his best and most promising leaders, but because of the edict, Daniel was sentenced to death and thrown into the lion's den.

God protected Daniel throughout the night. To the king's dismay and relief, Daniel was alive and unharmed. I have heard people pray, "Give me faith like Daniel." That is a bold prayer indeed! Given enough time, we will all face our own lion's den moment. When that happens, it is my prayer that I too will have faith like Daniel.

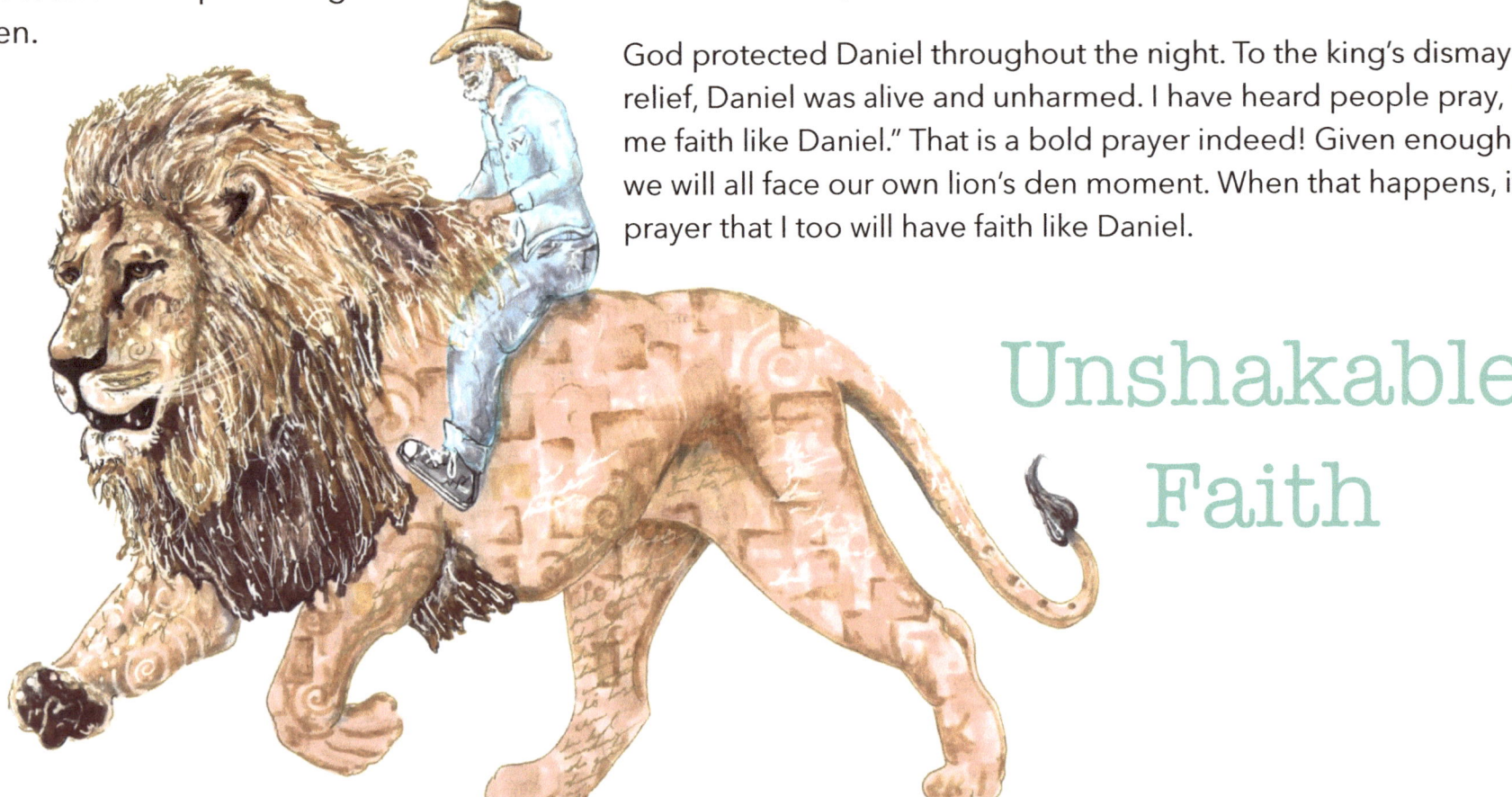

Unshakable Faith

Following a Star

As I worked on this drawing, I found myself realizing how little I look up at the night sky. Historically, stars and constellations were relied upon for navigation.

Challenge: Tonight, step outside and look up. Take a moment to consider just how crazy awesome our night sky is.

Question to Consider: How often do you miss something simply because you are looking or spending time in the wrong places?

"Now after Jesus was born in Bethlehem of Judea in the days of Herod the king, behold, wise men from the east came to Jerusalem, saying, "Where is he who has been born king of the Jews? For we saw his star when it rose and have come to worship him.""
Matthew 2:1-2 ESV

Spread your Wings

American artist Donald Featherstone is renowned for creating the iconic plastic pink flamingo in 1957. Regardless of personal opinions about this art piece, it's undeniable that his design—based on *National Geographic* photos—played a pivotal role in turning the flamingo into a cherished and beloved symbol.

A lesser-known fact is that all flamingos possess black flight feathers, which are enriched with melanin, resulting in a deep coloration and enhanced durability due to the keratin layer, akin to human fingernails. These remarkable feathers not only enable these magnificent birds to take flight but also shield their wings from the wear and tear of life's journeys.

This reflection prompted me to ponder a deeper truth: much like the flamingo's inherent ability to soar and its resilience, we too are not designed to be mere static adornments in the yard of existence. Rather, we are created and equipped by God to spread our wings, embrace risks, share love, and serve one another.

"As each has received a gift, use it to serve one another, as good stewards of God's varied grace:"
1 Peter 4:10 ESV

Resources

This verse has always fascinated me. It is simple yet so very true. God has placed everything we need on the earth—not just to survive, but to thrive. Food, fuel, water, building materials, and precious metals were all part of His plan. Everything conceived by man has been constructed from raw materials that were readily available.

"Look at the birds of the air: they neither sow nor reap nor gather into barns, and yet your heavenly Father feeds them. Are you not of more value than they?"
Matthew 6:26 ESV

Explore

Today, I will see Yosemite for the first time. The anticipation and sensory tingle of exploring a new place is magical. I imagine heaven as a place where we never stop discovering just how amazing, creative, and good our Creator is. Earth is simply an appetizer for the glories we will experience in the next.

"For since the creation of the world God's invisible qualities—his eternal power and divine nature—have been clearly seen, being understood from what has been made, so that people are without excuse."
Romans 1:20 NIV

Thrive

Rainbow trout, originally native to a small corner of the Pacific Northwest, have found their way across the globe, flourishing in diverse waterways and becoming a staple of fish farming. However, there's a crucial caveat—they cannot survive in polluted waters!

In fact, rainbow trout have been relied upon to verify water quality in many water treatment centers.

In a similar way, we tend to thrive in diverse ecosystems and environments, but just like the rainbow trout, we wither quickly when we find ourselves immersed in the polluted, dark, and difficult places of life.

I am grateful that I have not had to fight this battle alone—

"Come to me, all who labor and are heavy laden, and I will give you rest. Take my yoke upon you, and learn from me, for I am gentle and lowly in heart, and you will find rest for your souls."
Matthew 11:28-29 ESV

Covering

Rhinos are tough, and when provoked, they can charge head-down at 30 mph. Although tough, they are intolerant of excessive heat, so you will often find groups of rhinos, known as a "crash," hanging in the shade or wallowing in mud.

In this world, things can get hot or out of control really quickly. I am thankful for God's steadfast love and grateful to walk in the shade of His covering.

"The Lord is your keeper; the Lord is your shade on your right hand. The sun shall not strike you by day, nor the moon by night."
Psalm 121:5-6 ESV

King of Kings

Dinosaurs are captivating creatures, though some steal the spotlight more than others. This week, I found myself sketching the king of them all – *Tyrannosaurus rex*. Paleontologists have unearthed fewer than 100 T. rex fossils, and only about 30 a partially complete. The most famous of them, *Sue*, was discovered in 1990 with 250 of her 360 bones intact – the most complete T. rex ever found. But what do we really know about *Sue*? Only what her bones reveal. We can estimate her height, length, and power – but her coloration, habits, and intelligence? Pure speculation. Bottom line: *Jurassic Park* took some serious creative liberties.

Reflection: There are far fewer hard facts about T. rex than I expected. Conversely, digging into another of my favorite kings – Jesus – reveals a wealth of historical information. Setting the Bible aside for a moment, Jesus was confirmed and written about by:

- **Josephus** (Jewish historian, *Antiquities of the Jews*, ~AD 93)
- **Tacitus** (*Annals*, ~AD 116)
- **Pliny the Younger** (*Letters*, ~AD 111)
- **Suetonius** (*The Twelve Caesars*, ~AD 121)
- **The Babylonian Talmud** (AD 200-500)
- **Mara Bar-Serapion** (letter written ~AD 70)

Not bad for one man who walked the earth for just 33 years.

Now pick the Bible back up, and we can discover even more – Jesus's habits, his beliefs, his teachings, and his character. We know what he liked to eat, who he ate with, what he stood for, and what he died for. We know that death couldn't hold him – and we can discover what that means for each of us.

Now, to answer the question you're all wondering: **Could I really ride a T. rex?** – Unlikely… but the jury's still out.

Love your Neighbor

As I hike trails, ride chairlifts, mountain bike, and navigate the streets of my hometown, I encounter people from all walks of life. I've taken up the habit of carrying stickers—created from my artwork—in my pocket. My goal is to give at least one away each day.

This practice has helped me meet many people I might never have encountered otherwise.

Jesus gives us some simple yet life-changing advice: "My command is this: Love each other as I have loved you." (John 15:12 NIV)

We encounter people each and every day—ask yourself: *Who is Jesus putting in front of me, and how can I show them a little love today?*

A Time to?

What time is it? Have you ever been stuck in a rut—spending time weeping when maybe you should be laughing, or mourning when God is calling you to dance? It is easy to become stuck or tied to an event or emotion. Ask yourself: What season is God currently leading you into?

"a time to weep and a time to laugh, a time to mourn and a time to dance,"
Ecclesiastes 3:4 NIV

Ordinary People

I started thinking the other day: What if Jesus had come at a different time? Who would He have called to be His disciples? The answer: He would have called similarly unlikely people. He selected ordinary individuals to usher in the extraordinary. This still happens today. He extends invitations to regular, ordinary people like you and me. We simply have to be willing to step out in faith.

"While walking by the Sea of Galilee, he saw two brothers, Simon (who is called Peter) and Andrew his brother, casting a net into the sea, for they were fishermen. And he said to them, "Follow me, and I will make you fishers of men.""
Matthew 4:18-19 ESV

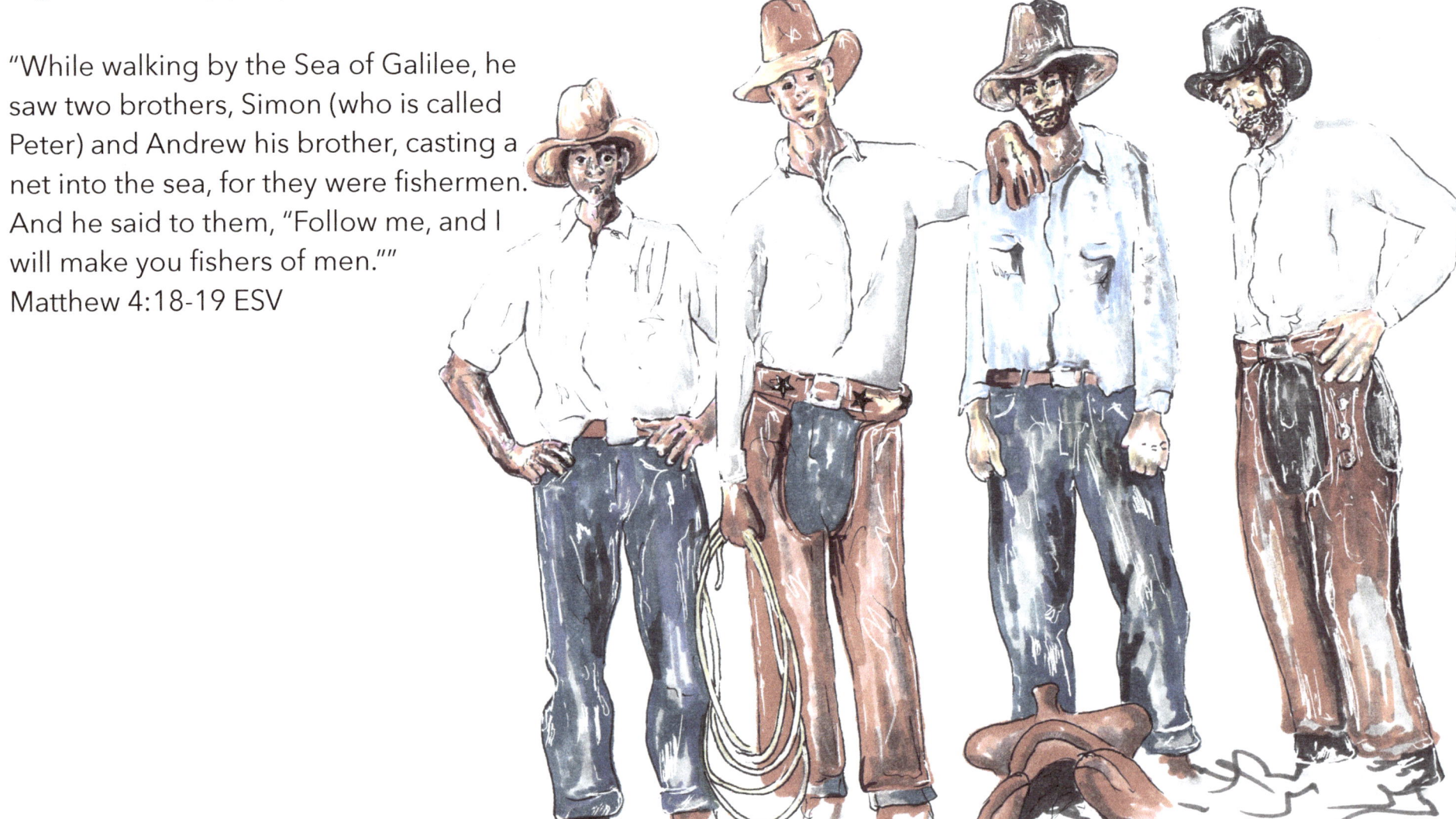

Drawing From a Place of Undeniable Hope

Undeniable hope - it's the kind of hope that refuses to be extinguished, no matter the circumstances.

"May the God of hope fill you with all joy and peace as you trust in Him, so that you may overflow with hope by the power of the Holy Spirit." (Romans 15:13)

Hope is not just wishful thinking. When it comes from God, it cannot be contained—it will overflow. It is unshakable because it is rooted in something greater than ourselves.

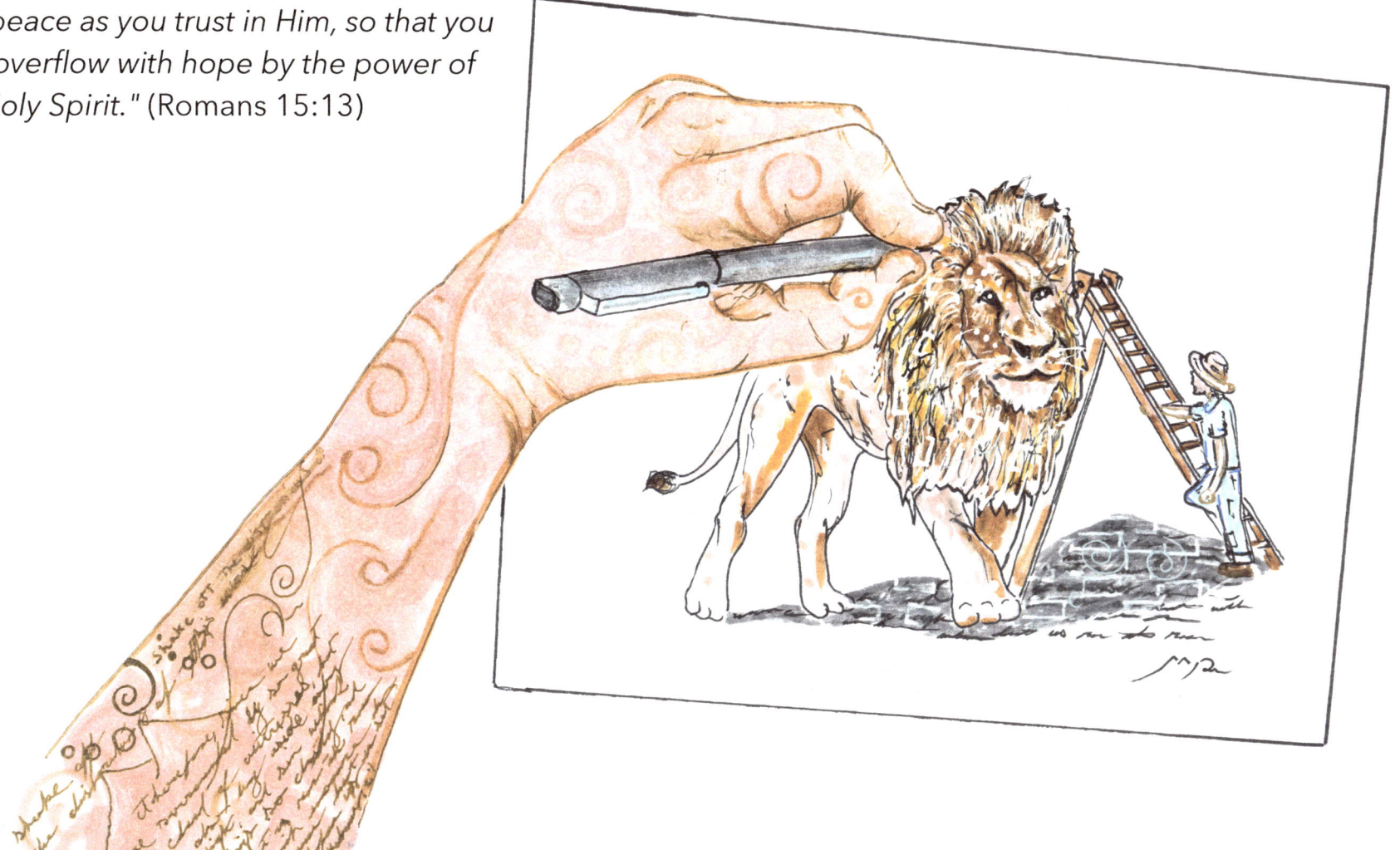

THE WRAP - This book is titled One Thirty Three One. Inspired by Psalm 133:1 "How good and pleasant it is when brothers dwell in unity". I thought it would be fitting to include 133 drawings and one testimony. Thank you for taking this journey with me. If you would like to see more of my work, Please visit 133ONE.com

TESTIMONY - *I was raised going to church. My mom made sure we never missed a Sunday, regardless of where we were. Even if we were camping, she would scrub our faces and drag us to the closest church she could find.*

As a young child, I believed what I was taught in Sunday school, but as most kids do, began to question as I grew a bit older.

As a teenager, I rebelled briefly, testing the waters by experimenting with alcohol. This led to a terrible rollover accident that, only by the grace of God, didn't result in three teenage fatalities.

This was a wake-up call for me. I rebelled in a different direction by attending multiple youth groups each week. It was on one of these nights that I heard Ken give his testimony and introduce the concept of a personal relationship with Jesus.

I'd say this was the point in my life when I "bought the fire insurance"—I accepted the idea of salvation, thinking that even if I were wrong, I'd at least have lived a good life.

In my early twenties, I married Lynda. We got a bit more serious about God and spent nearly a decade working with high school youth on Sundays, Wednesdays, and Thursday nights. This was more than just life insurance, but I still wasn't fully sold out.

In my thirties, I became a father. That's when God really began working on my heart. I was no longer satisfied with a simple insurance plan, but I wasn't sure where to start.

Up to this point, my Bible reading had been sparse, rare, and mostly a shotgun approach. I prayed a simple prayer: "God, if You are real, I want two things. One, give me a love for Your Word, and two, show me You are real in a unique way."

God is so creative, and He loves a good challenge. He drew me closer to Him through art. This journey has continued for the last 15 years. Through it, I've seen God speak in crazy ways. It took me to Haiti, Colombia, Brazil, and Peru, and gave me a love for His Word that I never thought possible.

My forties were filled with adventure with my family and marked by significant growth in my faith. I had the honor of baptizing both of my boys, each during an evening service at Journey Church.

I had reached a point in my walk with God where I knew He was real, I knew He loved me, and I knew He expected me to faithfully love others. I believed that if I obeyed God and followed the rules, everything would work out. I spent a lot of time planning for the future—college for my boys, family trips, retirement, and more.

But on April 30, 2022, our family's life changed forever. That day, while surfing the river wave with my 17-year-old son, Ben, my world came to a screeching halt. Ben fell and didn't surface. His foot got caught between two plates on the mechanism that actuates the wave. Ben was underwater for six minutes. He wasn't breathing and had no pulse when we finally freed him and got him to shore.

Paramedics met us and immediately started CPR. Ben was transported to St. Charles, where they continued to fight for him. After an hour with no pulse, the doctor approached Lynda and me to let us know that despite their efforts, he wasn't responding.

We were allowed to be in the ER with him, and we continued to pray. I held Ben's hand, squeezing it three times—a gesture in our family that always meant I love you. Ben squeezed back. I told the doctor, and he silently watched. At that moment, Ben's heart began to beat, and he started breathing on his own. We were moved to the ICU.

In the ICU, we were given 24 precious hours with our son after he had been pronounced dead. This incredible gift from God allowed us time to let Ben know just how much we loved him and how proud we were of the man he had become. We read to him and prayed over him. On May 1st, we lost Ben due to multiple complications.

Ben lived and loved hard during his short time on this earth. He impacted many lives, and Lynda and I are proud that God chose us to be his parents. Ben will be fiercely missed, but we rest in the assurance that he is not just in a better place—he is in the best place. We have now invested half of our worldly fortune in heaven and look forward to the day we are reunited with our son.

It's often said that God won't give you more than you can handle. That's a nice sentiment, but the reality is that tragedy will come. When it does, God doesn't just walk alongside you—He carries you through the storm. I can testify that the loss of our son is far more than we could handle on our own. God has carried us and still is. We are forever changed by this experience and realize now more than ever that time is a precious gift, and it's much shorter than you think.

Assurance of Eternity - Our lives can change in a moment. If you would like the assurance of eternity, here's some good news: it is a free gift—and just a prayer away.

Before you pray, take a moment to reflect. Think about the people you've hurt and those who have hurt you. Consider the times you've been less than honest—when you've compromised, lied, or cheated. Acknowledge these moments, and then release them to God. Remember, Jesus has already paved the way, paying the price for your transgressions. Ask God to help you let go of the hurt, pain, anger, and anxiety you carry. Be honest—God already knows everything you've done.

Now, pray:

Lord Jesus, thank You for the gift of salvation. I repent of my sins and surrender my life to You. Wash me clean and make me new. I believe You are the Son of God, that You died on the cross for my sins, and that the grave could not hold You—for You rose again. Lord, I am grateful for this gift of salvation and commit to seeking You every day. Amen.

Romans 10:9 (ESV): "Because, if you confess with your mouth that Jesus is Lord and believe in your heart that God raised him from the dead, you will be saved."